This Game Called
HOCKEY

This Game Called HOCKEY

Great Moments in the World's Fastest Team Sport

Ross R. Olney

Illustrated with photographs

DODD, MEAD & COMPANY   NEW YORK

Copyright © 1978 by Ross R. Olney
All rights reserved
No part of this book may be reproduced in any form
without permission in writing from the publisher
Printed in the United States of America

1 2 3 4 5 6 7 8 9 10

Library of Congress Cataloging in Publication Data

Olney, Ross Robert, 1929–
    This game called hockey.

    1. Hockey.   2. National Hockey League.   I. Title.
GV847.O55   796.9′62   77-16872
ISBN 0-396-07524-X

*To Pat and Amy Wills
and their sons, Dick and Tom*

Contents

	Introduction	11
1.	A Goal-Scoring Machine	17
2.	Hockey Is Fighting	22
3.	The Night They Were Going to Shoot Howe and Lindsay	29
4.	Has a Goalie Ever Scored a Goal?	33
5.	The Secret Weapon	39
6.	A Long Hockey Game	43
7.	The Silent Fans	48
8.	Talk About Quick Scoring	56
9.	Hockey's Explosive Night	61
10.	"I Never Thought About *Not* Playing"	68
11.	Hockey Fans Help Win Games, Too	74
12.	The Longest Game of All	78
13.	Maurice Richard vs. Killer Dill	82
14.	Are Hockey Players Superstitious?	87
15.	Eddie! Eddie! Eddie!	91
16.	The Golden Jet	96

17.	The Rocket's Goals	100
18.	Eddie Shore and Ace Bailey	106
19.	Penalties, and One That Was Asked For	111
20.	Hockey Has Some Nice Guys, Too	117
21.	Hull's 51st Goal	122
22.	The Least Expensive Hero in Hockey History	127
23.	Out of the Dressing Room and into the Penalty Box	132
24.	Orr!	137
	Index	142

Acknowledgments

The author wishes to thank the following for photos, advice, encouragement, and hockey anecdotes: Dan Avey, excellent hockey analyst; David Bier, photographer; Cleveland Barons hockey club; Detroit Red Wings hockey club; Bob Miller, one of the best announcers in the business; Montreal Canadiens hockey club; Minnesota North Stars hockey club; Lou Nanne, a fine hockey player; New York Islanders hockey club; New York Rangers hockey club; St. Louis Blues hockey club; Vancouver Canucks hockey club; and especially M. H. "Lefty" Reid, curator of the Hockey Hall of Fame, for taking the time to help when I really needed it, and hockey buddies Wayne and Lorraine Pinkstaff.

Protect the goal at all costs! Ranger goalie Ed Giacomin waits for the attack, unaware of another Ranger already in the net.

Introduction

HOCKEY IS a tough game. But it is also a beautiful, flowing, exciting game of color and grace. Each team is a blend of bright uniforms and fast action, all made especially radiant by the gleaming white ice on which the players work.

Yes, hockey is rooted in violence, injury, and bloodshed. All of these are a part of the rugged game, where all players wear razor-sharp knives on their feet and carry clubs in their hands. It is a hard game for participants. It is a game said to have the most difficult of all scores to make. Getting the six-ounce, inch-thick, frozen rubber puck into the four-by-six-foot goal is a frustrating task for the attackers. Keeping it out is just as frustrating for the defenders.

That, in spite of what first-timers often see as little more than a band of men zigging and zagging about on the ice, is the sum total of the game of hockey. Get the puck in the goal. If you do that more times than the other team, you win. If you allow them to do it more often that you, you lose.

Although both teams are skimming and curving gracefully (or not so gracefully) back and forth on the ice and the referee and two linesmen are raising arms, making signals and blowing whistles, hockey is just that easy to understand. Sure, the "unstoppable" game stops often, but only for penalties or serious injuries. Otherwise it goes on to the end of the time period. Even substitutions are made "on the fly." The new players come on when the tired players reach the bench.

What happens on the ice during this exchange? The other team scrambles to score.

Forgetting the whistles then, the idea of hockey is to get the puck in the net. Usually this can be done by any means at your disposal, *not* short of violence. It is perfectly legal in hockey to slam your shoulder or hip into an opponent as he streaks down the ice with the puck. Such a "body check" generally sends him sprawling or crashing into the sideboards

A hard body check sends both players sprawling to the ice.

or endboards, sharp skate blades slashing and twinkling in the rink lights.

It is legal to take the puck from him by almost any technique you can devise on the spot. You can sweep it from him or poke it from him with your stick; you can check it from him or lift his stick up off the ice; you can crash into him and hope it skips away to one of your teammates; you can shout at him to distract him or you and others can gang up on him.

If *you* have the puck you can attempt to get it in the enemy goal by almost any means. You can bring your stick up and hit the puck like a golf ball with a "slap shot." The puck will speed toward the goal at a lethal rate, yet relatively unprotected defensemen will gladly fall in front of it to stop it before it reaches the last line of defense, the goaltender. They will willingly stop the puck with body, arms or legs, or even head or face if there is no other way.

You can get closer and flip the puck into the net with a "wrist shot." You can hit it again the instant it bounces off any player with a "rebound shot." In the violence around the goal mouth, you can poke it, bump it, hit it, bounce it, slide it, flip it, shout at it, hit it in like a baseball, or do almost anything else to get it in. You cannot kick it in, but you can cause an opponent to kick it in by bouncing it off his foot or skate, and that is just as good a score for you.

Professional hockey players are *tough*. In many professional sports the players are college graduates with other professions to back them up when they retire, or fail in sports. Of course there are also hockey players who are professional men, but as a general rule hockey players come up through a series of leagues to the top. They start as teen-agers, or even as children, and hockey becomes their *life*.

They are, at the top, stitched together and wired up. During their battle to the best-paying teams they often acquire hundreds of stitches in face and body, and broken bones are part of their game. Some reach the heights to become sports heroes.

One player who had almost no formal education at all was New York Ranger Eddie Shack, a rough-and-tumble battler on the ice. Shack reached the top. He felt the way to play the game was to simply overpower the opponent. But his lack of education was a sore point and other teams took advantage of this. One time Shack was moving the puck up the ice past the opponent's bench. The enemy coach leaned out.

"G'wan, stupid, you can't even *spell*!" shouted the coach.

Shack dodged around a defenseman, shot the puck toward the goal, and though the goalie made a desperate grab, it skimmed into the net. The red goal light flashed on.

Shack raised his stick in triumph, then skated happily back up the ice. As he passed the enemy bench, he stopped and leaned over to the coach. Then, like a child reciting a lesson in school, he said, "Goal . . . G-O-A-L . . . *goal*."

Hockey is *exciting*. Often one team or the other must play "short-handed" because a penalty has removed one of their players from the ice. But that doesn't mean *everything*. The great Bobby Orr once made a goal and assisted on another while his team was skating short-handed. You never know.

So forget the penalties and the "whys" of them and watch the action. Each team wants to score and will go to almost any extreme to do so. The techniques of the game and the calls of the referee are easy to understand and will come to

He shoots! He scores! Paul Holmgren of the Philadelphia Flyers scores against the Los Angeles Kings' goalie Rogie Vachon.

every fan with watching and listening to the game announcer.

What you want to see is a goal!

One of the great hockey announcers, Bob Miller of the Los Angeles Kings, says it best.

"He shoots! He *scores*!"

Every time it seems one of hockey's great moments.

But then, in the history of the game of professional ice hockey, there are particular great moments that forever stand out. They can happen any time, at any game, and they could depend on who happens to be witnessing them. You could logically feel that a winning effort by the home team is a great moment, but the opponents might not be expected to agree.

You might have a favorite player, one not so beloved by other fans, so what you see him do is more likely to be a great moment to you. A great moment can be anything to anybody. Often they are come-from-behind victories, special efforts by players, overcoming injuries to play, last-second wins or losses, playing through heavy penalties, or some other great individual, team, or even fan effort.

Here, then, are a couple of dozen great moments as selected by one hockey fan. Some happened years ago, some are more current. If you are a hockey fan you probably have a list of your own, but chances are some of these will be on your list. If you are not yet a hockey fan, you might consider using these as your own until you build some favorites, as you surely will while watching the marvelous game.

For ice hockey is truly one of the most exciting games of all.

[1]

A Goal-Scoring Machine

A HOCKEY GOAL is said to be one of the most difficult scores to make in all of sports. Time after time the speeding puck is turned away by the goaltender, who with his pads and gloves and stick can cover a large percentage of the goal mouth by just standing there. And he *doesn't* just stand. He twists and leaps and sprawls and reaches out and hits with his stick and smothers with his body. He comes out of the goal to challenge players, cutting down the angle of the shot, then backs quickly to cover accidental rebounds.

Not that some odd goals haven't been scored in hockey. One player fired a long shot at the goal, then skated to the bench as a new line of players came onto the ice to take over. Meanwhile a defensive player accidentally touched the puck with his skate, tipping it over the goaltender's stick and into the goal. The rules say that the last offensive player gets credit for a goal knocked in by the defense. So for the first time in the history of hockey (and the *last* time) a player on the bench scored a goal.

There was another record about to be set the night of November 7, 1968, at the Spectrum in Philadelphia. On the

St. Louis Blues team was Red Berenson, a player who had spent several years shuttling back and forth between major league and farm clubs until he was sold to the New York Rangers by the Montreal Canadiens in the early sixties, and then to the Blues.

Though he had played in thirty games for the Rangers, Berenson didn't score a single goal. So a hockey player who had moved his family forty times in the six previous years prepared to move again. He was tempted to just move out of hockey altogether, but he decided to keep trying.

Then the Rangers sold him to the Blues and the history-making night came closer. Berenson scored some goals in St. Louis, but the 1967-68 season started very slowly for him. He just couldn't seem to get going. Eventually Berenson became one of the most valuable players on the Blues' team, but during this period, though he would score an odd goal here and there, he was having a difficult time.

The Blues checked in to play the tough Philadelphia Flyers that night, but Berenson didn't seem to be doing any better than before. During the first period of the game he shot but missed several times. In the back of his mind was probably the thought that he would soon be moving again—if any other club wanted him.

Then, late in the first period, he stole the puck for a clean breakaway towards the Flyers' goal. It was being guarded by ace goalie Doug Favell.

Defenseman Ed Van Impe was between the streaking Berenson and the goal, but Berenson swerved to the right, faking Van Impe out of position. At the same instant Favell, crouched and tense, glided out to meet him. Berenson flicked his wrists with a backhand shot and the puck lifted inches

Red Berenson of the St. Louis Blues scores the first of six goals during a game with the Philadelphia Flyers. Goalie Doug Favell sprawls in an attempt to stop the shot.

over Favell's stick. Into the goal it went.

Berenson lifted his own stick high in the air as his team-mates pounded him on his back. The goal had been a long time coming and it felt *good,* though Flyers' fans were groaning.

Berenson had no idea what was going to happen in the next forty minutes.

In the middle of the second period he managed another breakaway, and again he beat Doug Favell for a goal. That made two for the game and in the back of his mind was the possibility of a "hat trick"—three goals in one game—after his long drought. It would be good for the team and it would look very good on his record.

Five minutes later he got the hat trick, three goals, something many players try for all their hockey career and never achieve. Once started, Berenson was becoming almost impossible to stop. He had fired the puck from the blue line, it hit the post, and in a crazy bounce ricocheted past a frustrated Favell. Red Berenson was ecstatic, waving his stick in the air, skating about the ice as even the Flyers' fans were cheering his accomplishment. His teammates rejoiced with him. If a hockey goal is difficult, a hat trick is near impossible. Berenson skidded into the goal to grab the puck as a souvenir, for it was the first hat trick of his career. He couldn't have even dreamed it at the time, but he wasn't finished with the Flyers yet.

Less than one minute later, before astonished Flyers' players and fans, Berenson shot number *four* into the goal. It was with a quick wrist shot after a perfect pass from teammate Camille Henry. Now the St. Louis bench was emptying to pound Berenson's back and wave sticks with him. Spectrum fans were thundering their own congratulations, for they knew that Doug Favell was an excellent goaltender being honestly beaten that night.

With moments left in the second period, Berenson skated across the center line, lifted his stick and burned a blistering slap shot at Favell. By then Favell must have felt like a man before a firing squad. He reached out desperately but he was too late. The puck was already dimpling the back of the goal net. Berenson had number *five*!

Finally finished? Not yet.

In the third period of a game that was turning into a rout

because of one player, Berenson grabbed the puck in still another breakaway. Faking one way, he shot hard at the goaltender. Again the puck skimmed into the back of the goal behind a shattered Favell.

Six goals! A *double* hat trick!

Berenson had tied the modern National Hockey League record for goals scored in a single game. Only Sid Howe of the Detroit Red Wings had managed the feat and that was back in 1944. Before that it had not been done since the 1920s, when hockey was played by different rules.

Not one of the six goals had been scored against a short-handed team, either. Every one was "honest." St. Louis beat the powerful Flyers by a final score of 8-0, though the Blues didn't need any more than Red Berenson that night.

[2]

Hockey Is Fighting

A HOCKEY FIGHT is a brawl, in most cases. There have been some fine and physical ones over the years in hockey, and from them could come certain rules of play. Especially now that the "third man" rule is in effect. The first man to step into a fight between two players, even if he sees himself in the role of a peacemaker, is more heavily penalized than the first two. Sometimes he is even ejected from the game.

So most modern hockey fights are between two players. It can be said with reasonable certainty that:

1. The man who gets in the first punch usually has the advantage.

2. If you are going to fight, be first to fight.

3. Flicking the glove in the opponent's face, then hitting him with the other hand before he can see it coming, is excellent strategy.

4. Balance is essential on ice, so fighting with short, quick jabs and not long-reaching haymakers is better.

5. The meaner you are, as a general rule, the easier it will be for you.

6. Nice guys finish last.

The most penalized player in the National Hockey League, Dave Schultz, now with the Pittsburgh Penguins, is surrounded by Montreal Canadiens during a goal crease fracas.

Though it has softened some, modern hockey is still rooted in violence and blood. All other things being equal, the meanest team will win. The team with the killer instinct will prevail.

One of the most famous fights in the history of hockey was also one of the quickest. It happened on a cold 1959 February night in the old Madison Square Garden in New York. The hockey game was between the New York Rangers and the Detroit Red Wings.

Most hockey teams have an "enforcer," a player who will jump in and fight anybody for any reason. Intimidation, pro-

Hockey fights are common on the ice. Players drop their heavy gloves and start swinging, or attempt to pull the other player's jersey over his head to hamper him, as shown here.

tecting smaller players, removing the other team's stars from the lineup, for whatever the reason, these players are sometimes better at mixing it up than they are at playing the game.

The Rangers had a notorious enforcer by the name of Lou Fontinato, a player who enjoyed his reputation as hockey's bad boy and undefeated heavyweight champion. He skated on the ice as though praying for a fight, with an air of braggadocio that struck fear into opponents' hearts and awe in the younger Ranger players. Fontinato was good, but he was best at enforcing. He would not only hammer an opponent until he was bleeding, he would then gleefully point out the damage he had done to the vanquished man as he was being led off the ice to a doctor. Lou Fontinato was always spoiling for a fight to improve his reputation even more, it seemed.

On this night in 1959, Gordie Howe, the superb Detroit Red Wing leading scorer, collided hard with his Ranger shadow, Eddie Shack, behind the net. Gordie had a reputation as a player who wouldn't take much from an opponent either, a fact that Shack could testify to from previous meetings. Shack had taken many raps from the stick of Howe, but this time it seemed that further violence was going to be avoided. Just as both men were getting back to their skates, the whistle blew and action should have ended. Referee Frank Udvari, who went on to become Supervisor of Officials for the NHL, was on the scene and all was calming.

But in the meantime Lou Fontinato was charging in from the blue line. He was in a *rage*. One of his teammates had been downed and retribution was going to be his.

"I want him!" he shrieked, "I want Howe!"

"Hold on, Lou. Use your head," warned Udvari.

"I want him," Fontinato repeated.

Udvari stepped aside and Fontinato charged ahead. He was probably remembering a couple of personal scores he had to settle with Howe. Howe had once almost sliced Fontinato's ear from his head in a game and there had been other bumps and bruises. Besides, if he could once-and-for-all finish off the superman from Detroit, one of hockey's all-time great players and a hard fighter himself, Fontinato's supremacy would be unchallenged.

His plan was to surprise Howe, a tactic that had often worked for him with some of the other tough players in the league. Hit first and hardest; get them before they could muster a defense. Howe, who was paying more attention to what might be coming from Shack, didn't notice the wild charge of Fontinato.

Chop! Chop! Fontinato belted Howe once, twice, again, chop!, sending him reeling.

But not down, and *not* intimidated.

Regaining his balance, Howe reached up, grabbed Fontinato's sweater front, and jerked him forward. Then he hit him square in the middle of the face.

THWACK! It sounded like an axe striking wood. Blood spurted from Fontinato's suddenly misshapen face. It was obvious that his cheekbone was broken. His nose was a bent mass. Several teeth were hanging and two just fell out as Fontinato's mouth dropped open in stunned surprise.

Clop! Howe hit Fontinato with another short jab. Clop! Clop! Fontinato was out on his feet, his face an ugly mass of blood and torn flesh. His nose was turned at right angles to his face.

Finally the linesmen, until then avoiding the sharp blows,

Lou Fontinato after his fight with Gordie Howe. His nose is bent, front teeth are missing, and he is bloodied and bruised. But the Rangers won the game anyhow, 5–4.

stepped between the two players and shoved them apart. Howe skated back to his bench, Fontinato was helped to his.

From that instant on it was downhill for Lou Fontinato, the enforcer. In his own mind disgraced by his showing, he was no longer the tough guy of the league. What was worse, he seemed to have lost his drive and ambition to be so. His play skidded down as well, and so did the fortunes of the New York Rangers. The unusual end-of-season collapse of this contending team was traced directly to the fight between Gordie Howe and Lou Fontinato.

Finally, Fontinato was traded to the Montreal Canadiens, but things didn't improve for him. His career ended in a flash when he was sent crashing into the boards of the Montreal Forum in 1962. Plastic surgery had repaired his injuries from the fight with Gordie Howe, but this time his neck was broken.

Always a tough fighter, Lou Fontinato fought back once again. The broken neck did not kill him, but he never played hockey again.

Fans of the game still wonder what might have been if Lou Fontinato, a tough and valuable hockey player, had decided not to attack Gordie Howe that night several years earlier.

[3]

The Night They Were Going to Shoot Howe and Lindsay

HOCKEY IS AN intense game, so constantly exciting and color-ful that it brings out the best and worst in players and fans. Players will battle each other until blood stains the ice, then turn around and fight each other to protect one who has been downed from *either* team.

Fans will boo, catcall, and even throw debris at a player or official who has angered them, then turn around and give a standing ovation for a player from either team who has made a particularly skillful play. At Canadian rinks, where fans have had many years to learn the sophistications of hockey, it is not unusual for an opposing goaltender to get a standing ovation for a series of outstanding saves against the home team.

But then in Canada or any other ice rink in pro hockey, the fans might turn around and boo the same keeper for making some bad moves in the net.

But on the night of March 24,1956, at least one follower of the game went beyond simple booing or tossing debris.

It was during the first round of the Stanley Cup playoffs

29

between the Detroit Red Wings and the Toronto Maple Leafs, two fine hockey teams. Detroit had home ice advantage for the first two games, and they won both. But during the second game Red Wing Ted Lindsay fought hard with Leaf player Tod Sloan. Then, later in the game, Red Wing Gordie Howe body-checked Sloan into the boards and Sloan was carried off the ice with a broken shoulder.

The Stanley Cup series was over for him, and the hopes of winning the Cup had been dimmed for the Maple Leafs.

The series of games then moved to Toronto where Maple Leaf fans were waiting, upset by what had happened to one of their best players down in Detroit. A real "get even" attitude had spread through Toronto. Not only were the Leafs down by two games, but the fans felt that Detroit had been playing dirty. Feelings were running high after one day's layoff between games for travel.

On the morning of the third game a man who refused to identify himself, for obvious reasons, called a Toronto newspaper. He repeated his threat over and over again.

"Don't worry about Howe and Lindsay tonight. I'm going to shoot them if they play in the game."

By the time the Red Wings arrived at Toronto Gardens for the game, everybody in town knew about the death threat. One Toronto newspaper had even printed a giant headline that told the story in a few words.

Will Shoot Howe, Lindsay to Avenge Sloan Is Threat, said the banner.

Assassins and threats from assassins became more commonplace as the world became more complex, but in 1956 such a threat was something to be seriously considered by all concerned. Extra police were added to patrol the Gardens and all suspicious packages that might contain a firearm were inspected.

Both Gordie Howe and Ted Lindsay were offered the chance to pass up the game in view of the threat, but both refused. In fact, locker room banter among the Red Wings centered on the two and their possible immediate demise.

One Red Wing player suggested that both Howe and Lindsay skate at the far end of the ice, as far from his position as possible . . . just in case. Another player with a more macabre sense of humor devised a plan that was to him almost perfect. On the team was a rookie player by the name of Cummy Barton, a player not yet in the class of either Howe or Lindsay.

The plan was to have poor Cummy wear Howe's number 9 on the back of his shirt and Lindsay's number 7 on the front. Then Barton was to skate up and down the ice to see what would happen.

Only one Red Wing violently opposed this plan in the locker room that night before the game.

Yes, it was Cummy Barton.

More jokes flew about, but underneath was the gnawing worry that the threat was more than just a crank call, that there might actually be a deranged hockey fan waiting out in the night to kill two of hockey's top stars. Quietly, Howe called his ill mother in Saskatoon, Saskatchewan, to assure her that he was fine and that she shouldn't worry.

Lindsay grew more and more angry about the matter as game time approached.

By the start of the game, both players were resolved that nothing in the world would keep them out of action. Still, their nerves were tight as they skated onto the ice (which could be exactly what the crank was hoping for).

The game was a hard-fought battle. Howe scored early, but by the middle of the final period the Leafs were leading 4-3. Then Lindsay, near the end of the game, as if to show that the threats had not bothered him, scored the tying goal.

In the first overtime period, Lindsay scored again, winning the game for the Red Wings (who won the series 4 games to 1).

To be a pro hockey player you need a superego, the stamina of a bull, and a total lack of fear. So what did Lindsay do after his final overtime game-winning goal? Bringing his stick up to his shoulder in a rifle motion, he skated around the rink shouting, "Rat-ta-ta-ta-ta-tat . . ." over and over again.

Ted Lindsay (far left) scores in overtime and the Detroit Red Wings win during the death-threat game. Gordie Howe is at far right. Other players are, from left, Mark Reaume, goalie Harry Lumley, Eric Nesterenko, and Jim Thomson.

[4]

Has a Goalie Ever Scored a Goal?

"HOW WOULD YOU like it if you were a business executive and every time you made a little mistake a red light flashed on and 18,000 people screamed at you?"

The question was asked by Jacques Plante, originator of the modern goalie mask and one of hockey's all-time goalkeepers. Such was the life of a goaltender in hockey.

Another great goalie, Glenn Hall, once said, "Having a goal scored against you is like getting your pants taken down in front of 15,000 people."

"Hockey is the most primitive sport," said Dr. Lloyd Percival, Chief Psychologist of the Canadian Fitness Institute of Toronto, "and goaltending is the most underdeveloped position in the sport."

Goalie Gump Worsley said, "When you're out there on the ice the only real friend you have is 200 feet away in the other net. Everyone else is your enemy."

Even your own teammates, meant Worsley. A puck can glance off their skates and into your net. Your own teammates can also injure you in a goal crease jam-up.

Ace goaltender Rogie Vachon of the Los Angeles Kings is tensed and ready for the puck if it should come his way during a face-off in a game with the tough Montreal Canadiens.

Goalies are slammed, hit with pucks traveling at race car speeds, cut by sticks and skates, and broken by goal posts. Their muscles are torn and their joints bent the wrong way. They usually leave the sport of hockey with stitching holding their skin together and wires and pins holding their bones. The whole point of the game is to slam the puck past a goalie. If he is slammed in the process, well, that's hockey.

The forward line gets a chance to shoot and shoot at the

enemy goaltender. Even hockey defensemen like Bobby Orr have become high scorers in the game. If any offensive players blow a goal they can grab the puck and try again, or they can take out their frustration in other fast action. They can run an opponent into the boards with a hard body check. For them, hockey is a fast-moving game with constant motion and flowing changes of opportunity.

The goalie must just stand there, braced and ready for the next onslaught he knows is coming.

In a few seconds they'll be back, happily slap-shotting the puck at speeds up to 120 miles per hour, with not a care whether they hurt him and only great joy if he fails in his job. They'll jam up in his crease and try to force the puck past him; they'll take advantage of every single one of his suspected weaknesses; they'll try to trick him, to outthink him, to be braver than he is, to overwhelm him.

They'll smile pleasantly at him, flicking the puck back to a teammate just when he thinks they are about to shoot, then bounce the puck past him as he turns to the new threat. For the first man has shielded the shot from him until the last split second. They will even try to ricochet the puck off his own goal posts, or, to his own great embarrassment, off his own skate.

They'll do *anything* to get the puck in the net. Then they'll skate away with their stick held high in triumph as the crowd cheers (or boos the net minder, if the game is at home). Tending goal in professional hockey is not one of life's serene occupations.

Nor is it a job where you have a chance to "get even." No, you must just stand there waiting, knowing what is about to happen to you. Perhaps that's why some goalies get sick be-

fore every game, and why others have retired at an early age to go into a more sane occupation, or asked to be sent down to the minor leagues where the pressure isn't so great, and *hang* the cut in pay.

Has *no* goalie *ever* had a chance to score against an enemy in a major league hockey game?

Modern goalkeepers are wandering farther and farther from the net to decrease the angle for a successful shot on the goal, and most goalies skate behind the net to help their team control a puck. Occasionally a goalie shoots the puck up the ice to a teammate.

Ken McAuley, who eventually became a fine goalie in the National Hockey League, once had a chance at a goalie's dream. While tending goal for the Edmonton Maple Leafs in the Canadian Junior Hockey Division in 1938, he was called. His team had just been awarded a penalty shot, a play in hockey where a player gets a free shot against the opposing goal with only the goalie on the ice to defend. Everybody else from both teams must take positions far from the play along the sideboards.

The Edmonton coach, to everybody's surprise, called on his own goaltender, McAuley, to take the penalty shot.

"Go ahead," said the coach with a grin. "You have one coming."

So goalie McAuley took off his padding, lined up against the enemy goalie, and prepared to shoot. He skated forward from the blue line, aimed his shot with great care, and *fired*.

"I thought I had the goalie beaten," he said.

In a few seconds they'll be back, and the poor goalie must start all over again to block the shot. Here Lou Nanne of the Minnesota North Stars badgers the goaltender.

What happened on that one and only time a goalie ever had a chance to score?

"The danged thing hit the post," lamented McAuley.

Another NHL goalie came even closer in 1977. Rogie Vachon, goalkeeper for the Los Angeles Kings, had blocked a shot just as a penalty was called in a game against the New York Islanders. At the same instant, Islander goalie Glenn Resch started for his own bench and teammate Bryan Trottier swept the puck up the ice. The puck skimmed past other Islanders and past a startled Resch into the net. The goal was awarded to the last defensive player to touch the puck (Vachon)—until after the game when a review of the video tape showed that Kings' player Vic Venasky had really been the last one to touch the puck.

And to this day, though it would probably give a big lift to all but the one who was scored upon, never has a National Hockey League goaltender ever scored a single goal in a game.

[5]

The Secret Weapon

THEY SAY THERE is nobody as devout as a new convert, and the faithful fans of the amazing Philadelphia Flyers hockey team proved the old adage true. The Flyers were an "expansion" team, a club put together when the National Hockey League decided that more hockey teams were needed. Often an expansion team is made up of new players not yet proven and older players who might have already seen their prime.

That didn't matter to the fans in Philadelphia. They loved their new team of Flyers with a passion. Not only that, but they supported the team at the box office, and tickets were always difficult to get.

The Flyers played a tough and rough brand of hockey, one that reminded many fans of the earlier days in the game. Coach Fred Shero taught his players to "take the shortest route to the puck, and arrive in poor humor."

Shero felt that the way to win hockey games was to keep the opposition flat on the ice, to intimidate them and keep them worried that you might hit them over the head with a stick. Shero's teams were always one of the most heavily penalized in the league.

But with this attitude, and with players like Bobby Clarke, Rick MacLeish, goaltender Bernie Parent (who proudly displayed a bumper sticker with a fan's slogan that said ONLY THE LORD SAVES MORE THAN BERNIE PARENT), and Dave Schultz, the most penalized player in big league hockey, the Flyers won game after game.

In fact, this new team in hockey went all the way to the Stanley Cup finals in 1974. All they had left to do was to beat the Boston Bruins in a best-of-seven series of games. The Bruins were one of hockey's original, and best, teams. It couldn't have been a tougher assignment for the young Flyers.

But they had something besides their fine players and great spirit, a "secret weapon" they used only when the chips were down, when they simply *had* to win a game. It was a seldom-used recording, played only before "must" games, and a strong part of the team's tradition. In hundreds of games the record was played only 39 times. The Flyers won 35 of the 39.

Never used lightly or with frivolity, the recording was kept in reserve through the first five games of the playoff series that year. Miraculously, the Flyers had won three. They needed to win only one more of the next two games to win the coveted Stanley Cup, something the world of hockey did not believe was possible. Not only that, but the next game was to be fought out in the Spectrum, on the Flyers' home ice. Then the series would shift for the last game, if needed, back to Boston.

Most of the Flyers and their fans felt that the upcoming game was the key. If they won, they would win the Cup. If they lost, the series would go back to Boston and they would

The Philadelphia Flyers, shown here in a goal crease altercation with the Los Angeles Kings, are the only expansion team to have won the Stanley Cup. They did it with a "secret weapon."

have lost their momentum. The next game was really a "must" game.

But the secret weapon, a stirring rendition of "God Bless America" sung by ardent hockey and Flyers' fan Kate Smith, was not used. Although nothing could be more vital than the Stanley Cup, and although the players wanted and needed to win that final game at home before the loyal fans who had supported them so faithfully, the record stayed on the shelf.

A new, improved secret weapon had been found.

The Spectrum did ring and reverberate that night to the great voice of Kate Smith singing the lucky "God Bless America," but it was not the recording. Instead, it was the real voice of the singer, for Kate Smith herself strode to center ice. She sang as never before the anthem that seemed to bring good fortune to the Flyers. She *hurled* the fine song across the Spectrum ice with great emotion and love. The beautifully patriotic words seemed to hang in the air as the melody swept the packed stands.

Many Flyers, caught up in the magnificent singing of the song, wept, and so did thousands of fans. Then Kate Smith moved from player to player, wishing them well, whispering to some, hugging them, during a ten-minute ovation from the fans.

Did the new improved secret weapon work?

The Philadelphia Flyers are the only expansion club in hockey's history to have won the Stanley Cup. For on that night the aroused team battled the fighting Bruins in one of the toughest games of the year. Bernie Parent, with mighty efforts, turned away 30 Bruins' shots. Meanwhile, Rick Mac-Leish scored a goal for the Flyers on a power play. It was the only goal of the game.

And the Stanley Cup came to Philadelphia, a new, young team. Also the best team in hockey that year, thanks to fine players, loyal fans—and a secret weapon that came to life.

[6]

A Long Hockey Game

A HOCKEY GAME is sixty minutes long. It is played in three 20-minute periods with rests between. During the regular season a game can end in a tie. In fact, teams win a place in the season-end playoffs by a points system compiled according to how many games they won (2 points for each), how many they tied (1 point for each), and how many they lost (no points).

There are no ties in the playoffs, though. The chips are down. The teams that make it into the battle for the Stanley Cup must play against each other until somebody wins, no matter how long it might take.

So a game that ends in a tie in regulation play in the playoffs must go into "sudden-death overtime." Regular 20-minute periods are continued, but only until somebody scores. At that point, the game ends and the scoring team wins.

In the spring of 1933 the playoffs were being fought out between the top teams in the league. In one such game the defending champion Toronto Maple Leafs had battled the Boston Bruins for three difficult periods but the score was still tied 0-0. The crowd was excited as the teams skated onto the ice for the first overtime period. Both teams were charged up and ready to end the game in a hurry.

But at the end of the first overtime period, in spite of a number of chances by both teams, the score was still 0-0.

At the end of the second overtime period the score was *still* 0-0.

The third overtime period? Yes, it was still 0-0.

By then the players had battled each other an extra 60 minutes, an entire extra game, and they were growing more and more tired. Hockey is a demanding sport. One sports-writer sat on the bench with a team of professional hockey players. He was surprised to see that as each shift came off the ice after only a couple of minutes of play, they were gasping and near collapse. Hockey players recover quickly for their next shift, but on the ice they must skate and play at the peak of their ability and that is demanding on mind and body.

This 1933 game ground on, with play becoming more and more ragged by exhausted players. Not that the game was unimportant. It *was*. But the players were getting near the limit of their endurance.

A fourth overtime period, 20 minutes of hard skating and bruising body-checking, brought no goal and the period ended with the score at the same monotonous 0-0.

The fans remained in their seats with a growing feeling that what they were seeing was impossible. Yes, a hockey goal is one of the most difficult scores to make in all of sports, but these teams had played nearly 2½ hours. These were some of the best players in hockey. Yet no goal had been scored.

The team coaches got together and approached the league president about postponing the game until the next night.

A hockey game is sixty minutes of action in three 20-minute periods. Only in the playoffs will the game go into sudden-death overtime.

Schedules would have to be rearranged, but they explained that the players were so tired it was possible nobody had the *strength* to score a goal. They could be there all night long, insisted the coaches. Word came over the public address system about the plan but the fans wouldn't hear of it. They had come to see either the Leafs or the Bruins win. The Leafs could go on in the playoffs if they won. The Bruins could stop them and possibly go on themselves if *they* won.

With the roar of disapproval over the plan from the fans, the president shook his head and the fifth period of overtime play began.

It ended with the score still 0-0.

How about just flipping a coin, asked the coaches? *No*, roared the fans, though the players were by then more than willing. Well, then, how about reducing the number of players on each team one by one until *somebody* scored? It is a fact that four on four and even three on three could produce more goals than the normal five on five.

No, shouted the fans.

The exhausted players sagged on the bench, awaiting the next suggestion.

Ah hah! The league president himself had an idea. How about playing the next period *without goaltenders*? Surely somebody would score and then everybody could go home.

Boo! said the fans. They wanted to see a hockey game, and hockey included men in the nets. Besides, both teams felt that this was going too far, and rejected the plan along with the fans.

So the sixth overtime period of the long game started.

Then it happened. Maybe the Leafs were thinking of the great silver cup, the trophy most say is more difficult to win than any other in professional sports. They had won it the year before. They would win it again, perhaps, if they just tried a little harder.

Four minutes and 46 seconds into the sixth period, after a total of more than 164 minutes of exhausting hockey, the Leafs slipped the puck past a sprawling Bruins goalie, and the game ended. It had been the longest game in the history of hockey to that time.

The toll on both teams was terrible. Maybe the Bruins were the lucky ones. They got to go home and rest after the players dragged themselves off the ice.

And pity the poor winners. The Leafs were no match for the refreshed New York Rangers only a few hours later. They struggled through the game, but the Rangers beat them handily and went on to take the Stanley Cup from Toronto to New York.

It was ten long years before Toronto won it back.

The Silent Fans

SOME DOCTORS SAY that it is possible for a person to die of a broken heart. In a time of great and enduring sadness, it is possible for a person to simply give up and let go their grip on life.

On a list of the all-time great hockey players, the name of Howarth "Howie" Morenz, the famous Stratford Streak, is certain to appear. Morenz was not a large man, but he worked at skating and hockey playing as a youth and was outstanding as a player for the junior league Stratford Club. At twenty he became one of the youngest players ever to sign a contract to play professional hockey.

The team that signed him? The mighty Montreal Canadiens.

Morenz was a hard-charging, devil-take-the-hindmost type of player who paid heavily in injuries for his wild and exciting charges up the ice to the enemy goal. He was beloved by hockey fans for his uninhibited style of play. Often he would merely plow into an opponent rather than try to skate around him.

He was small in stature, but Howie Morenz, as a rookie

player, led his team to the Stanley Cup in 1923. As a beginner he helped his team win the trophy most difficult to win in all of sports. Twice more he did the same thing. He was that good.

But eventually the injuries began to tell on him. More than once he had to be carried unconscious from the ice. After ten years of being the star of the Canadiens, his muscles were sore and his reflexes slowing. Younger players were being signed on, players who were fresh and strong and yet to feel the cruel cut of the stick or the painful tearing of muscles. Morenz' goals scored began to drop. In the 1932-33 season he scored only fourteen goals, a low for him (though in those days teams played far fewer games than they do today). The next year his total dropped to eight. He tried harder and harder but his body was failing him.

Then one night in 1934 his humiliation was complete. He skated onto the ice at the Forum and the fans, hometown people who once screamed his name and cheered for him, *booed* him. It was the final straw in the downward slide of Howie Morenz. His confidence left him completely. He was crushed. That same year he was traded to Chicago.

He played poorly. He was traded to New York. Nobody wanted the former superstar. He was too old, they said. He was washed up as a hockey player. He was a bum.

Morenz himself felt that he was indeed at the end of the road. Though barely thirty-four years old, he felt like an old man.

But Montreal hired back Coach Cecil Hart, Morenz' coach during his fast-shooting, Stanley Cup-winning years of 1930 and 1931. The coach remembered the great Stratford Streak and the wild charges up the ice that had many fans calling him "The Canadian Meteor." Montreal needed a star like that again. So, although he was by then thinking of leaving the game of hockey forever, Morenz was traded back to Montreal, back home. He should have been happy, but he was almost too embarrassed to skate.

"You can do it, Howie," insisted Hart. "Keep trying. Keep trying. You *can* come back!"

Howie Morenz *did* try. Montreal fans waited and watched as he fought back. He was first to arrive for practice and the last to leave. He was a dedicated player. Gradually his sheer determination began to affect the other players and Montreal began to win games. On the ice Morenz' great speed and carefree style of play was coming back. His stickhandling improved until it was like that of the old days.

Morenz began to feel young and confident again. Sitting alone in the Forum between practice sessions, staring down at the sheet of ice, he would recall the early days when he so loved the game of flashing skates and blurred pucks that he would do almost anything to play.

When he was a boy, his mother had arranged for him to take piano lessons. But every Saturday morning on his way to the teacher's house he had to pass the frozen river where the other boys were playing hockey. He was heartsick.

Still, for a couple of weeks, Howie attended the lessons. He finally learned one piano exercise by heart, and every Saturday afternoon he would practice the exercise at home. Over and over again he would play the same notes. This went on for weeks. Every Saturday morning he would leave home with his music.

Finally Howie's mother, concerned that he wasn't progressing as fast as she had hoped as a piano player, visited the teacher.

On any list of all-time great hockey players of history, the name of Howarth "Howie" Morenz would have to rank near the top.

"Howie has been playing the same notes for weeks and weeks," the mother complained. "When are you going to advance him to something new?"

The piano teacher gave Mrs. Morenz a blank look. "Howie . . .?" she asked. "Howie who . . .?"

Only then did Howie's mother realize that the boy had long since given up the piano lessons on his own, and was back at the river doing the thing he loved the most.

Sitting there in the darkened Forum, Morenz grinned at the memory. At practice he continued to work harder than anybody else.

And he won back the job as first line center on the team, the second time in his life he had done so. Howie Morenz had come back. Harder and harder he charged. The Canadiens were back in first place because of him and he intended for them to stay there. He loved his new life with a desperation.

"Morenz! . . . Morenz! . . . Morenz! . . ." chanted the fans, driving him on just like years before. To them, he was once again the superstar on the greatest team in hockey.

But then, on January 28, 1937, came the game against the Chicago Black Hawks. Streaking toward the Chicago defensive zone in typical fashion, Morenz leaped toward a Hawk. Some say it was a ridge in the ice, others say an enemy stick found its way between the skates of Morenz. He tripped and slammed full force into the end boards. His leg was shattered.

For weeks he lay in the hospital, a heavy cast from hip to foot, knowing he would never again play his beloved game of hockey. He could no longer be a Canadien. This time he was *really* through. There would be no coming back from this.

Yes, the doctors said his leg was healing. He would recover in time, but no, he would never play again.

On March 8, 1937, in the early morning hours, not long after a report that said he was recovering, Howie Morenz suddenly took a turn for the worse.

Then came the news from the hospital that shook the sports world. "Howie Morenz is dead."

The official report on "The Canadian Meteor," the Stratford Streak, who set record after record and who made a magnificent comeback after many said he was through, was that he died of a heart attack following a nervous breakdown.

But those who love hockey say it was that Morenz just didn't care to live without the game, and that he really died of a broken heart.

As loud as hockey fans can roar, they can also be a very quiet group. All of Canada and the hockey world was shocked at the untimely death of the great Howie Morenz.

How could Howie have died? They had said he was recovering from the broken leg he had suffered on the ice. Yet Morenz had died and Canada went into mourning. The official funeral was to be held in Montreal, for the first time ever on the ice of the Forum where the Stratford Streak had played in his greatest games.

So he lay in state at center ice, the player who was called the *beau sabreur* (dashing cavalryman) of hockey. Morenz was to hockey what Babe Ruth was to baseball, A.J. Foyt to auto racing, Pelé to soccer, and Kareem Abdul-Jabbar to basketball. He was the top star, the best of all.

He had been noted for the awesomeness of his breakaway charges. He would *thunder* down the ice with complete abandon, worrying not a bit about his own health or the health of any other player. It was on such a rush that he had

53

Morenz' funeral in the Forum before the "silent fans."

crashed into the St. Catherines Street endboards of the Forum.

Morenz had been a happy Montreal Canadien who dressed the part of a sports hero and lived the life of one to the fullest. He was known for pranks like throwing huge fire-crackers under police crusiers in traffic. He enjoyed life.

And then, perhaps because he knew he could never play hockey again, he died.

The great names in hockey were taking turns standing as honor guards around his bier day and night there at the Forum. On the morning of the funeral one sportswriter arrived to find the front doors completely jammed with fans awaiting entrance. Realizing that he could not fight his way through the crowd, the writer turned around and walked to the furnace room entrance. The he went down the passageway to the Closse Street entrance to the ice.

The silence was eerie. He was accustomed to hearing the screaming of packed stands as devoted Canadiens' fans cheered the home team on, but this silence was overwhelm-

54

ing. It was probably the fact that a funeral was soon to be held, and that Howie Morenz was at center ice for the last time.

Soon the Forum would begin to fill with sad hockey fans. At that moment, though, the sportswriter thought only of Howie Morenz alone on the ice with his honor guard. Ahead, through the entrance, he could see the lonely little group and the casket.

He shivered. He felt cold and suddenly very alone himself. He stepped out onto the ice and then his sadness was truly overwhelming.

For only then did he realize that he was not alone. In the seats, mourning the great hockey player, unmoving and in silent tribute, sat more than 15,000 people.

[8]

Talk About Quick Scoring

ODDLY, IT HAD been only three days before that Bill Mosienko of the 1952 Chicago Black Hawks remarked to a pal how nice it would be to have your name in the NHL record book. At that time Mosienko's name was not in the books.

Then he exploded into action and etched a record into the books that may never be broken.

"I sort of caught lightning in a beer bottle," Mosienko modestly said later.

Unfortunately, since the game didn't mean much in the standings that year, with the Hawks buried deep in last place and the New York Rangers in fifth place, not many spectators were in the old Madison Square Garden. There were about 3,000 fans for the March 23 game.

But the Ranger fans were all very pleased with the way the game was going, for the Rangers were leading in the third period by a score of 6-2.

The Black Hawk line for the face-off was Gus Bodnar at center, and wingmen George Gee and Bill Mosienko. Defending the Ranger's goal was rookie goaltender Lorne Anderson. Anderson had done well up to that point, but he was about to be bombarded into the record book himself.

Bodnar controlled the puck at the face-off, shooting it into the Rangers' zone to Mosienko. Like a streak, Mosienko headed for the Ranger goal, dodging around Ranger Hy Buller. Quickly he fired a wrist shot and it skimmed into the net low on the right side in spite of a sprawling grab by Anderson.

Mosienko reached into the net, retrieved the puck, and skated over to the bench to hand it to coach Ebbie Good-fellow. He wanted to keep it as a souvenir.

The game then continued with another face-off at center ice.

Again Bodnar won the draw and fired the puck to Mosienko at the blue line of New York. Mosienko was already at full speed when the perfect pass hit his stick. Once again he shot around Buller and moved in on Anderson. Anderson braced himself for the shot he knew was coming.

Mosienko had beaten the young goalie on the right side once. He decided to try again. He twisted his wrists and sent the puck skimming along the ice. Anderson wasn't ready for the quick shot and it streaked past his outstretched glove into the back of the goal.

Mosienko lifted his stick high in the air, then skated over to retrieve another puck. It was his second goal of the night, but what was more exciting, it had come within 11 seconds of the first one. He was jumping as he skated back to the bench with his second souvenir.

Even the fans were cheering Mosienko's amazing two shots. Still, it was not a record. Back in 1931, Nels Stewart made two goals for the Montreal Canadiens against Boston in an astounding 4 seconds. In fact, Pete Mahovlich of the same

Canadiens has since made two goals in 5 seconds in 1971, and in 1972 Ralph Backstrom of the Los Angeles Kings made two goals in 6 seconds.

Once again the referee brought a puck to center ice for a face-off to begin play. Once again Gus Bodnar squared off. With more than thirteen minutes left to go in the game, Bill Mosienko was naturally dreaming of getting a "hat trick," three goals in a single game. But even he couldn't have imagined what was about to happen next.

As if a replay of the previous two face-offs, Bodnar won the draw. This time he flipped the puck to the left wing, George Gee. Gee and Mosienko both started into Ranger territory. As they crossed the Ranger blue line, Mosienko dashed forward. Gee saw him go and flipped the puck all the way across the ice directly onto Mosienko's stick.

That was all Mosienko needed. Though Buller was waiting with fire in his eye, Mosienko once again skimmed around him and skated in on Anderson. Poor Anderson was also waiting and this time he had made up his mind that no goal would be scored on the right. He moved in that direction just as Bill Mosienko decided to change his strategy. As Anderson moved, Mosienko lifted the puck into the empty left corner of the goal.

Only *10 seconds* had passed since the second goal!

Bill Mosienko had scored three goals in only 21 seconds. And that *was* a new record, a record that still stands in the hockey record books.

In the game of hockey assists are very important and add to the total points of a player. So, also in the record book is the name Gus Bodnar. He holds the record for the fastest three assists in history—in that same game, of course.

With Mosienko's three goals and two more in the third period by another player, the Black Hawks won the game with a final score of 7-6.

There are some final footnotes to the record happenings in this game. Gus Bodnar, who set up the three quick goals of Bill Mosienko and went into the record book for doing it, is in another "fast gun" section of the book. Under "Fastest Goal by a Rookie" is the name Gus Bodnar. While playing his very first game in pro hockey with the Toronto Maple Leafs, Bodnar took the opening face-off and slammed it into the goal in an astonishing 15 seconds. What a thrill for a brand-new rookie!

Bill Mosienko shoots the last of his three quick goals, all scored in only 21 seconds against the New York Rangers. Goalie is Lorne Anderson.

To make the record more interesting, it was the same New York Rangers he scored against.

Need more? There is a section in the record book head-lined "Most Assists, One Period." Remember how Bodnar assisted in the three goals of Bill Mosienko? Well, the name Bill Mosienko is listed in *this* section, with 4 assists during the third period of a later game between the Black Hawks and the Canadiens. He assisted Clint Smith of the Hawks, who is also in the book for the most goals scored in one period in the history of hockey.

Proving once and for all that hockey players may be rugged individualists, but the game is a team effort.

[9]

Hockey's Explosive Night

IT WAS A black day in hockey. Frenzied fan behavior can be seen at most hockey games, with shouts of derision at enemy players and particular venom directed at hapless officials who dare to make a call against the home team—which of course they must in the course of a game.

But that is generally as far as the majority of hockey fans go. Otherwise they are banded together by a mutual love of the rugged game. On this night in hockey, though, the matter went further—much further.

It started a few days earlier, on March 13, 1955, during a game between the great Montreal Canadiens and the battling Boston Bruins. The game was being played in the Boston Garden.

Fights on the ice are not at all unusual in hockey. A player checks another player into the boards during heated action and the checked player takes offense. Quickly gloves are dropped and the fists begin swinging. Seldom are players injured during these battles (they are hockey players, not boxers), and so most often the two linesmen simply stand back and watch, allowing the energy of the two fighters to wear down a little before they step in.

Modern linesmen finally jump in and pry apart the players. Meanwhile, the referee, who seldom becomes involved in such body contact, stands off and assesses penalties.

There were reasons why this particular fight began. First, in the game was the legendary Maurice "Rocket" Richard. He was playing with all his skill to achieve a record he had never before won. Though he was acknowledged to be one of the best, if not *the* best, hockey player in history, Richard had never won the single season scoring title. He had come close, and he was a consistently high scorer every season, but he had never been the single highest scorer in goals plus assists.

As his army of fans cheered him on, Richard knew that 1955 could be his year. Either he or his talented teammate, Bernie "Boom Boom" Geoffrion, would surely take the title. Richard wanted the honor, and with his burning eyes flashing almost pure hatred of the enemy goaltender, he would streak in and shoot at astounding speeds.

He was a quick-tempered player, instantly ready to defend any wrong or imagined wrong. So it happened on this night that he had a disagreement with Bruin player Hal Laycoe. In hockey most players punctuate their argument with a quick smack of a heavy stick across a foe's head. This is what Richard and Laycoe tried to do to each other.

Richard, a noted stickhandler, hit Laycoe several times. When another Bruin tried to restrain him, the Rocket hit him as well. Then linesman Cliff Thompson waded in to see what he could do to break up the fight, and he was slugged by Richard.

Hitting another player is a serious offense in hockey, one
that will draw an almost certain penalty. But hitting an official is unforgivable.

Richard was suspended by NHL president Clarence
Campbell after a meeting of all participants in the league
office.

Nor was this an ordinary suspension for a game or two.
Campbell's suspension of Richard was for the entire re-

A shocked Richard speaks to Canada during his suspension from hockey in 1955.

mainder of the season, including any Stanley Cup playoff games.

"I was never so shocked in my life," said an unhappy Richard. "I was numb from head to toe."

All of Canada was shocked as well. Hockey is the national game of Canada, and Richard was a national hero. How could Campbell do such a thing? Immediately the league president began receiving letters, telegrams, and phone calls, many of them unpleasant and some of them threatening.

Fans of the Canadiens took up petitions and submitted them to the Canadian government in the hope that a politician could help convince Campbell to lift the suspension before it was too late for Richard to win the scoring title he had sought for so long a time. But politicians didn't want to touch the controversy. One fan even telegraphed the Queen of England to ask for her intervention in the suspension.

Four days later, on March 17, the team returned to Montreal for a critical game at home. The stage for the infamous St. Patrick's Day riot had been set. Either Detroit or Montreal would go into first place with this game. Aroused fans streamed into the Forum to see if Campbell had weakened and decided to allow Richard to play against Detroit. No, the Rocket was not suited up. The suspension remained in force.

When Campbell arrived for the game, a brave man certain he was doing what was best for hockey, he was roundly booed by the packed stands. If the fans were in an ugly mood then, the mood darkened even more as the game progressed. One young fan walked up to Campbell and put out his hand as if to shake with the league president. But when Campbell reached out, the fan struck him hard in the face. Then several other fans joined in and finally a squad of police had to surround Campbell to preserve order.

On the ice things were no better from a Montreal point of view. With disturbances in the stands continuing, Detroit had taken an almost insurmountable 4-1 lead. The teams left the ice for the end of the period, then a smoke bomb exploded in the grandstands. Debris showered the ice from disgruntled fans. Then tear gas bombs hit the ice. The situation was growing more and more dangerous as the crowd became an angry mob.

Officials decided to end the matter. They awarded the victory to Detroit by forfeit. This really set off the fans. Angrily

they streamed out of the Forum to meet more thousands of fans outside who had not been able to get in to see the game.

A riot started.

While Campbell was being spirited away by police, fans began to smash Forum windows. Gunshots rang out. Many stores along St. Catherines Street were looted. When the riot subsided, the area around the Forum looked like a bombed-out war zone. It had been the worst riot in Montreal history.

Chagrined fans stole home, the fight out of them. And Campbell did stick to his guns. The suspension was not lifted and Richard's teammate, Geoffrion, took the scoring title.

Canadiens' fans love their team perhaps more than any other team's fans, but so great a favorite was Maurice Richard that popular young Geoffrion was actually booed on his own home ice when he accepted the scoring title.

A smoke bomb explodes in the Montreal Forum during the 1955 riot over Richard's suspension from the game. The game was forfeited to Detroit, and the riot spread for blocks outside the arena.

[10]

"I Never Thought About Not Playing"

SURE, YOU GET slammed around in many sports. Football is not an easy game and even players in basketball and baseball can be seriously injured. Other sports are rugged. Soccer is an extremely demanding sport, where players must run hard for many, many miles without relief during a game.

But hockey players are about the toughest of all. Not only are they hard as nails, but it is traditional in hockey for players to shrug off all but the most serious injuries and return to the game.

Yes, hockey players are tough. Bobby Baun of the Toronto Maple Leafs was hit with a stick and lay on the ice unconscious for so long that he was finally carried off on a stretcher with a concussion. Out for a month? A week? A *day*? He was back in the game that same night to score the winning goal.

One of the greatest players of all, Bobby Hull, had more than 300 stitches to close the cuts in his face. Goaltender Johnny Bower (who had a broken jaw, 250 stitches in his face, and all but two of his teeth knocked out or broken off during his career) once had an enemy player's skate slice into his face, hook around a tooth, and rip the tooth out through the hole. It was a terribly painful injury, but Bower stopped the shot.

Terry Sawchuk, one of hockey's all-time star goalies, had 400 stitches in his face, including three in his right eyeball. He had many broken bones and played with mononucleosis and a damaged spine that caused him to walk slumped over. A psychologist once said of Sawchuk, "He is on the edge of an emotional abyss, harried by flying pucks and suffering from a persecution complex."

Sportswriter Jim Murray once described Sawchuk as "a collection of fragments. He wasn't born, he was zippered. He looks like a statue that was shattered and put back together again." Yet Sawchuk was one of the best goalies in hockey history.

Eddie Shore had a total of more than *900* stitches in his face and body, acquired during his hockey career.

Hockey player Noel Picard walked into the trainer's room during a game with a bad cut on his head. The doctor got ready to wash up and don gloves but the trainer just handed him a needle and thread. The doctor shrugged, reaching for a pain-killing shot to give to the injured Picard.

"Just sew it up in a hurry, Doc," ordered Picard, waving away the pain-killer. A drug can affect a player's concentration, Picard knew, and he was going to play again that night.

The doctor did as he was instructed, sewing up the gash as quickly as he could. Then Picard got up from the table to go back onto the ice.

"You going to be around for awhile, Doc?" he asked as he paused at the door.

"I'll be here until the game is over," replied the doctor.

"That's good," answered Picard. Then he indicated the fresh wound on his head. "Because in about ten minutes the guy who did this to me is going to be down here to see you."

One of the toughest players of all had to be the Chicago Black Hawk's Whitey Stapleton, especially during one 1971 game with the Montreal Canadiens. The Black Hawks won the first game of the best-of-seven playoff series and were confident going into the second game. The third and fourth games would be played in Montreal. Chicago did win that second game, but Stapleton wasn't around at the finish.

The second period had started and Stapleton was skating as a defenseman for the Hawks.

When a team plays the Canadiens, winners of the Stanley Cup more times than any other team, they find that the game is often played in their own end of the ice for the most part. It is very difficult to get the Montreal team back to their own goal. They hound you, forechecking and pressing and shoving, and simply not allowing you to get a play started.

They push you behind your own goal, take away the puck, and shoot before you know what has happened. They are excellent passers, great skaters, and top shooters.

So Stapleton was busy during that 1971 playoff game. As a star defenseman he was called upon to work every minute of every shift.

Canadien Rejean Houle was streaking in for a shot and Stapleton dropped to his knees to block it. At that instant, Houle spun on one of his skates to change direction. But he was off-balance. One of his skates sparkled up, twisted, and as Houle went down the skate caught Stapleton in the face.

Just an instant after he has been terribly cut, Whitey Stapleton has leaped to his skates and continues to fight Rejean Houle (14) for the puck.

Hockey skates of the forward line are sharpened regularly, often between every period, depending on the player. The edges of the blades are like a razor to permit quick stops and precise turns.

The skate went through Stapleton's lip, up through his right cheek and almost to his eye, laying open the entire side of his face. It was as if a surgeon had made the incision with a scalpel. For a moment Stapleton felt nothing, no pain or ache. Blood was pouring from his opened face, staining his uniform and the ice, yet both players jumped back to their feet to fight for the puck. Then a wave of shock hit Stapleton.

Knowing that he was hurt, he skated to the bench and as a substitute rushed into the game the Hawks' trainer, Skip Thayer, examined the gash. Stapleton was hurried to the dressing room, then Thayer put in a quick call for a plastic surgeon. Report to the hospital, ordered the doctor.

Whitey Stapleton always remembered the name of the doctor with amusement. He felt that the name fitted the situation, since his face looked to him like a road map for the next few weeks. The surgeon's name was Dr. Randall "Rand" McNally.

Dr. McNally used 52 stitches to close the gaping slash in Stapleton's face. Then he had to work inside, in the defenseman's mouth and around his lip. So he used 52 *more* stitches. At the upper part of the cut the doctor had to sew together muscles that had been severed. In all, Whitey Stapleton received more than 100 stitches for that one wound.

Finally the doctor finished. Stapleton's face had a long blue-grey line from eye to lip, held shut by black stitching. Have you ever had a few stitches? Remember how they made you feel: weak, unsteady, and ready to rest and regain your equilibrium?

Stapleton got up from the emergency room table and drove back to the ice rink to pick up his family, who had been there to watch the game.

The next morning he was back practicing with the team. When somebody asked him if he intended to play in the next game, he answered, "Heck, I never thought about *not* playing."

If he was hit in the face and the wound reopened, he reasoned that a doctor would be available to sew it shut again.

It was a tough series with many penalties to kill and a great deal of hard skating, but Whitey Stapleton played in *all* of the remaining games. With the series tied at three games each and Chicago ahead by two goals in the final, deciding game, Montreal roared back to win.

But Whitey Stapleton was there fighting to the bitter end, his face a fearsome sight but his spirit and skill undimmed.

[11]

Hockey Fans Help Win Games, Too

SPORTS FANS are a special breed, and hockey fans are unique among sports fans. They can sit quietly stewing about a game going wrong until suddenly, without warning, they can explode into thunderous cheers or boos. They understand the game of hockey as well as the officials, and are quick to point out any error on the ice. Hockey fans will stand for no bullying of their home team players, yet will cheer a home team enforcer as he belabors an innocent visiting player.

A fan, regardless of his love for the old home team, will loudly voice his displeasure when the team is struggling, or making mistakes.

That's one of the reasons why the Los Angeles Kings were worried about skating out on Forum ice after a disastrous road game in Boston. They had gone into the 1976 playoffs with a remote chance of eliminating the Big Bad Bruins, but Boston needed only one more win to eliminate the struggling Kings. With the best-of-seven series tied at two wins each, the Bruins had smashed the Kings the night before in Boston. The final score of the humiliating game was 7-0. The Kings had played like a high school team against the smooth and polished Bruins.

Boston needed but one more game to move on and it didn't matter to them that the game was to be played in Los Angeles at the Forum. They were sure they could beat the fading Kings on any rink.

So, humbled and embarrassed, the Kings skated out onto the ice of the Forum before a full house of more than 16,000 fans. How could a team that had made it to the playoffs lose 7-0? As always, goaltender Rogie Vachon led the parade of Kings through the door. Then he weaved his way to the goal. The Kings looked chagrined to a man as they skated one by one from the tunnel to sweep past Vachon and tap his pads for luck. They looked beaten before the first face-off.

For a brief moment, just an instant in time, the Los Angeles crowd watched. Moments before they had been half-heartedly booing the Bruins who had come on the ice first. They had seemed almost disinterested. Their team was "down." The fans were "down."

Then, not one by one but as a single great thundering voice, like a loud clap of thunder, the crowd *roared*. The thunder filled the Forum, startling the players, silencing the organ music, stunning the broadcasters and public address announcers into quiet, shaking the very floor of the building. Nor did the great roaring stop as it had started.

The officials waited, the game waited, the National Anthem waited as the heartfelt cheering continued. It was impossible to hear a next-seat neighbor in the Forum. The players, lined up and ready to begin, dropped their heads emotionally. The cheering rolled on. Goaltender Vachon lifted his mask to wipe his eyes. The roar continued.

The Kings, goats in their last game and favored to lose and be eliminated in the present one, raised their heads and looked at each other. On the ice and on the bench their shoulders seemed to straighten. A twinkle came back into their eyes. The thunderous cheer continued to shake the building.

For seven long minutes the great standing tribute to the Kings rolled on. Win or lose, the fans were with the team that night. It was one of the longest standing ovations ever for a hockey team, certainly *the* longest one for a team who had played like the Kings in their most recent game. It hadn't been set up by a slick public relations man. It was a spontaneous giving to a team by its fans.

Throughout the game the crowd supported the Kings with loud applause. The team was struggling against an excellent Boston team, but fans continued their cheering. The Bruins were one of the best teams in hockey and the Kings were not, yet the support continued no matter what happened on the ice.

It would have been almost like fiction for the Kings to have smashed the Bruins into the ice, ground them down and soundly beaten them. Going into the third period of the desperate game the Bruins were leading by a secure 3-1. The Kings were playing at their peak, but still they were losing. Vachon made save after save of whizzing Bruin shots, but gradually the game was ending.

The crowd even then did not desert the Kings. With every single blocked shot, every check, every shot on the Bruin goal, they roared their approval.

Then the Kings' bow-legged little star Marcel Dionne shot hard at the Bruin goal and at the very last instant Mike Corrigan deflected the puck past Bruin goalie Gerry Cheevers. The score was 3-2. The crowd cheered lustily but no louder than before, for that would have been nearly impossible. Still the building shook.

Again Corrigan controlled the puck, but a hard body check sent him sprawling near the Bruin goal. Twisting, laying on his back in front of the crease, he reached out with his stick with a sweeping move. Cheevers reached at the same time but Corrigan's stick bumped the puck. It riccocheted off the goalie's stick and into the net. The game was *tied*. Moments later, the horn blew to end regulation play.

The same deafening roar greeted the Kings as they charged back onto the ice for the start of overtime. It was a new game. The fans, by then hoarse from cheering, thundered on through the opening face-off.

With only two minutes gone, the Kings' Butch Goring and Tommy Williams streaked up the ice on a two-on-one break. Goring shot just as defenseman Brad Park slid hard into him, sending him spinning on his stomach. The puck skimmed across the short span of ice, hit the goal post, and rebounded into the net past a desperate Cheevers' reach.

The Kings had won the impossible game, tied the series, and forced the playoffs into a final game in Boston. A new wave of thunder shook the Forum as Goring was carried around and off the ice by his happy teammates.

Hockey fans are indeed a unique breed.

"I don't know but what the fans deserve the victory as much as we do," said Marcel Dionne, a Kings star and one of hockey's top shooters.

"The fans [in other cities] are great, but this was something special," said Kings' Frank St. Marseille. "I've never seen anything like it. I couldn't believe it. I know we all felt it."

The Longest Game of All

ON MARCH 24, 1936, in Montreal, the Montreal Maroons were playing the Detroit Red Wings in a playoff game. No ties. It was a tough, hard-hitting game of hockey with both teams excellent on defense and both goaltenders razor sharp.

At the end of regulation play, sixty minutes of bone-bruising hockey, the score was 0-0. The players were still sharp and ready to play and the fans were more excited than ever. "Sudden victory," as some fans call it, is an unnerving brand of hockey. A goal can be scored in an instant, from anywhere on the ice, with not a bit of previous warning, and it is all over. There is no tomorrow in this type of hockey.

No, the fans didn't mind. They were ready for another period. It was almost like getting more than your money's worth to see an extra period of hockey for the price of a standard three periods.

If they had only known.

The fourth period was fought out and still the score was 0-0.

But in the words of an earlier day hockey hero, King Clancy, the game was still being played "joyously." It was

Clancy who explained away his many hurts with a laugh and a quick, "I was never *really* injured."

Then Clancy went on. "Sure, I lost teeth and busted my nose four or five times, but I mean injured so I had to miss a game. I guess I've had a hundred stitches in my face but I was never what you'd call good looking. I always thought hockey was . . . well . . . a *joyous* kind of game. I always said you never get hurt as long as you play recklessly. You reel with the punches. I'd go into the fences like a rag doll, not all tensed up. I just didn't care. That's how the game was played then."

And that is how the Maroons and Red Wings were playing in 1936, with a reckless abandon.

The fifth period resulted in no score. The sixth period was the same, and a few of the fans began to think of a game still fresh in their minds from only three years before. In that game the Toronto Maple Leafs had battled the Boston Bruins into the ninth period, the sixth overtime period, before a score. This game wouldn't go that long, but it was getting pretty lengthy.

The players were beginning to get tired and even a few of the fans began to hope for the end. Money's worth is one thing, but this game was getting *long*.

Not that the players weren't getting some good shots on goal. They were, but one thing or another would prevent a score. The puck would bounce off the goal post or take a bad hop and bounce over or around the net. The goalie would come out and smother the puck, or a defenseman would bat it away before it reached the crease. Both teams had shots on goal, but no scores.

The seventh and eighth periods passed.

Finally the *ninth* period of the game, the sixth overtime period, began. The teams had played 60 minutes of regulation play and 100 more minutes of sudden-death overtime, where the strain is especially great. The score was still 0-0. Yet everyone on the ice and every fan in the stands knew that the teams would continue to battle each other until somebody scored. It had to be that way. They wanted it no other way.

So nearly 10,000 fans in the old Forum in Montreal settled back for still another 20 minutes of hockey. Many of them probably didn't even realize that after 4 minutes and 46 seconds a new record was going into the books. They were from that moment on watching the longest hockey game in history.

But not for much longer.

As happens in these games, it ended quickly. Two minutes after the new record was set, after nearly three hours of solid hockey, the Detroit Red Wings' Hec Kilrea, a defenseman, scooped up the puck. Quickly he started up the ice toward the Maroons' goal. Alongside him was Detroit forward Mud Bruneteau.

As they crossed the centerline, Kilrea shot a pass over to Bruneteau. Maroons' goalie Lorne Chabot watched carefully, bracing himself for a shot as the Wings' players moved closer. Bruneteau, who had not been one of the better shooters on the Red Wings all season, skimmed around the last Maroons' defenseman and headed for the goal.

Fans tensed and leaned forward as Chabot came out of the crease and moved toward the flashing Detroit forward. Chabot was suddenly the last line of defense for the Maroons.

Bruneteau lifted his stick and slapped the puck hard.

Chabot made a diving reach to his right, but the puck slipped by and slammed into the net at the rear of the goal.

A great groan rolled down from the Montreal fans. Their team had lost, though their goalie had stopped an incredible 88 shots.

It was the 89th shot he missed, and it put him, and them, into the record book where they still remain today—along with the winning Detroit Red Wings.

[13]

Maurice Richard vs.
Killer Dill

MAURICE "ROCKET" RICHARD, one of the best players in the history of hockey, was also one of the game's toughest. It took hardly anything at all to set off the Rocket, star player for the Montreal Canadiens. You could look at him wrong and he might swing his stick. He had one of the shortest fuses in hockey. Richard, who was the cause of the St. Patrick's Day riot in Montreal in 1955, gave his very best every minute of every game.

"His eyes were all lit up, flashing and gleaming, like a pinball machine. It was terrifying to see him coming at you," said goalie Glenn Hall of Maurice Richard.

Some say he was tough in self-defense. Almost every single one of the all-time great hockey players have also been fighters. For hockey players from other teams seem to gang up on the stars.

Still, because he was one of the game's highest scorers, they seemed to gang up especially on the Rocket. Opposing teams drove him to distraction, whether he had the puck or not, with hard body checks, bruising stick action and, when they really wanted to risk life and limb, fists. They would bang and bump him around the ice and do anything they could to rattle him and break his concentration.

The Rocket could not bear to lose. Missing a shot was something he had to carry on his conscience until the next opportunity. With this attitude, he was very hard to stop once he started a charge to the goal, eyes gleaming and puck on his stick.

Many teams assigned particular players to shadow Richard and stop his scoring. Tony Leswick was such a shadow for the New York Rangers. In every game against the Canadiens, Leswick would hover at Richard's shoulder, poking, jamming, bumping, doing anything legal and some things not so legal to harass and bother the great Rocket.

But in one game Richard grabbed the puck and started for the goal. Leswick grabbed Richard's jersey to hold him back. Richard skated on, dragging Leswick behind. So Leswick rammed his stick into Richard's ribs. The pain stabbed through the Rocket's body but still he skated on.

Another Ranger, Gus Kyle, skated across to slam hard into the two players, tumbling them both on the ice. Richard went down first with Kyle on top of him and Leswick on top of Kyle. Only the Rocket's stick hand was free. Desperately he reached out from the pile of players, sweeping his stick at the puck.

It bounced into an unprotected corner of the Rangers' goal.

The New York goalie was angry at his teammates. "Why didn't you hold him?" he shouted.

Leswick smiled wanly as he pulled himself up from the ice. "What do you want me to do," he fired back, "tie him up?"

Game action finally reached the point, though, where

"It was terrifying to see him coming at you," said goalie Glenn Hall of the great Maurice "Rocket" Richard.

Richard's manager, Tommy Gorman, filed a formal protest with Mervyn Dutton, the National Hockey League president. Gorman claimed that other teams and players had informally created a "Wreck Richard" club.

"It is evident that players are sent on the ice only to trip, hold, block, or wrestle Richard by any means at all," wrote Gorman in his protest. "He can take care of himself in a stand-up fight, but they are trying to stop him by any means they can, legal or not."

Gorman officially asked the league president to order all referees to help protect his star player.

The protest was awaiting action in the league office when the Canadiens went to New York for a game with the Rangers.

It happened that the Rangers, in a desperate bid to stay in the race for the Stanley Cup, had acquired one of the meanest, toughest, most warlike players of all. Banned from the American Hockey League for being too hot-tempered and quick to swing a stick at an opponent's head, Bob Dill had been hired by the Rangers to stop players like Richard.

Dill, who had been trained as a boxer by his two pro-fighter uncles, was known as "Killer" Dill.

Nobody can say for sure who started it, but minutes into the game that night a fight broke out. Soon every player on the ice had dropped his gloves and started swinging at somebody else. It was a wild battle, with the crowd screaming for their favorite players and unhappy linesmen trying to calm the fighters without getting knocked down themselves. At the outset of the fight, Richard had spotted Dill just as Dill spotted Richard. Instantly they had skated toward each other.

Some hockey players believe in a little push and shove

before any serious hitting. Not Rocket Richard. As he skimmed up to the man he knew was there only to antagonize him, he knocked him flat on the ice with a roundhouse swing. Dill was that quickly unconscious on the ice.

Order was restored and both Richard and a groggy Dill were sent to the penalty box to cool off. But as Killer Dill's head cleared and he realized what had happened, he was furious. He looked around and there was the Rocket in the very same box, separated only by a waist-high wall. Dill reached across and gave an angry shove to Richard.

Instantly, without a moment's hesitation, Richard wound up and knocked Killer Dill unconscious again.

Shortly after, the protest filed by Gorman was rejected by the league president, who decided that Richard was well able to take care of himself under any circumstances and without help from the officials.

[14]

Are Hockey Players Superstitious?

PROFESSIONAL ATHLETES are as a rule somewhat superstitious, but hockey players take the cake. They fuss and scratch and skate in certain circles and tap each other. Many of them suffer from the dread Triskaidekaphobia, and others have Nomatophobia, Ailurophobia, Phonophobia, or even Entomophobia. Some have the very terrible Panophobia.

In the order lised, these are fear of number 13, fear of names, fear of cats, fear of noise, fear of insects and, finally, fear of *everything*.

Even the order in which they enter and leave the ice is of critical importance to many hockey players. Marcel Dionne of the Los Angeles Kings must be the last one on the ice for warm-ups and for the game.

Goaltender Rogie Vachon of the same team must be *first* on the ice (a tradition with net minders), if he is guarding the nets that night. But that's not all. When Vachon enters the locker room on game night, he first tapes his fingers with sponge. Then he straps on the forty pounds of equipment he wears in a particular order. Then the trainer hands him some

smelling salts to keep his head clear, followed by a stick of gum.

"I know it is stupid," admits Vachon in the French-Canadian accent that so many modern hockey players have, "but it has to be this way, from the same trainer, in the same order."

In the stands, Vachon's wife Nicole is wearing the same clothing, the same lipstick, the same shoes, even the same eyelashes, and sitting with the same friends in the same seat she was sitting in during the last winning game. If the Kings lose, she must change friends.

On some teams the players tap their goalie's pads once for luck, but certain players tap twice, or once and then twice, or in some other combination certain to continue the winning streak or break the losing streak.

88

Writer Dan Stoneking once described a particularly superstitious hockey player. The player was Louis Vincent Nanne,
a Minnesota North Star who didn't walk under ladders, hated
black cats to cross his path, and never failed to toss salt over
his shoulder if some were spilled. He was careful about han-
dling mirrors and avoided the number 13.

Then when the hockey season arrived he *really* got involved. Nanne had what he called his *routines*. It could be
said that Nanne carried superstition to an extreme never
reached by any other hockey player, though almost all are
superstitious to some degree.

On game day, for example, this is the complex set of superstitions followed by Lou Nanne.

1. He drives to the rink on a certain road, but he returns
home after the game on a different road.

2. On the way to the rink he listens to one radio station,
but when he arrives at the parking lot he switches to another
station.

3. Walking down the ramp to the dressing room he walks
outside the railing (but inside the railing as he leaves after
the game).

4. He arrives at exactly 6:25 for an 8:00 P.M. game and is
the first to finish dressing, at exactly 7:05.

5. He hangs some of his street clothes in one room, the rest
in another room.

6. His equipment, which has been laid out for him in a
certain order, is donned in a certain order, always in the same
sequence.

7. When the evening programs are brought into the dressing room, Nanne looks through one then passes it always to
his right. It has been said that his team captain, who dresses

to his left, has never seen a program.

8. Nanne won't lace up his skates until his captain laces his.

9. He never picks up his stick until a certain two other of his teammates have picked up theirs.

10. He always follows a certain teammate down the stairs to the ice. Once when that teammate was injured, Nanne was in a quandary until he found another teammate with the same initials as the first one. So he followed him until the first one recovered.

11. During warm-up he takes so many shots, skates in front of the goal so many times, and behind the goal so many times.

12. During the game, he never looks at the scoreboard clock, or checks for the scores from other games being played around the league.

13. He holds an ice cube in his hand until his own team gets control of the puck. If it melts before that time, he gets another one.

14. After each period of each game he walks into the dressing room and blows his nose twice. Not once and not three times, but exactly two times, even if he doesn't have a cold.

15. Then he walks back to his bench, but always between two particular wastebaskets.

16. There he sits down and unlaces five eyelets on each of his skates. He used to unlace only three, but "five makes me feel luckier," he says sincerely.

Nanne might carry his superstitions to an extreme but the fact remains that for whatever reasons he cares to believe, he is a fine and very valuable hockey player. Besides, most other hockey players are at least somewhat superstitious, a fact quite obvious to the fans at any game.

[15]
Eddie! Eddie! Eddie!

ONE OF THE fixtures on any team is the goaltender. He is the solid base upon which the team is built. You may never win any games if you do not have a good attack force, but you can never lose a game if the opponents cannot get a puck past your goalie.

The New York Rangers had Eddie Giacomin, a graying man of superb skill in the net. They had had him for the previous eleven years, and Madison Square Garden fans had come to admire and respect him. Eddie was always there when a critical save was needed.

Then came November 2, 1975, and Eddie Giacomin skated onto the ice not in the familiar Ranger uniform but in the bright red of the Detroit Red Wings. It was to the Wings' goal he skated and begun to fuss around in the ice of the crease as goalies do.

Less than two days before, Eddie Giacomin had been put on waivers and sold to the Detroit hockey club. The former Vezina Trophy winner (best goalie in hockey that year) was shocked and so were the Rangers' fans, but the trade had been made. As luck would have it, the first game after the

Goalie Eddie Giacomin as a Ranger

sale was with the New York Rangers at the Garden.

So there he was, under tremendous pressure as the enemy goalie in his own home town, on his own home ice, before his own home fans. What a thing to have to do! It was an experience that most professional athletes would have avoided and Giacomin was given the opportunity to sit the game out.

But in spite of the chance that he could be soundly embarrassed by his old team and get off to a bad start with his new team, Eddie Giacomin decided to play. He had no idea how he would be welcomed at the Garden as he skated onto the ice, but as he scarred the ice of the crease with his blades and shoved the snow this way and that, he began to hear the New York fans.

The cheers from the stands were gradually turning into a chant.

"Eddie! . . . Eddie! . . . Eddie! . . ." echoed through the Garden. The chants continued through the playing of the National Anthem. They built, shaking the building and overwhelming the players on the ice. These were Rangers' fans. They were chanting the name of the *enemy* goaltender.

Standing at attention before his goal, Giacomin finally broke down and wept. He turned to acknowledge the fans. Other players from both teams shuffled and grinned, flipping a wave or bouncing a stick in Eddie's direction. Wings and Rangers alike smiled for the man in the red suit in the Wings' goal.

"Eddie! . . . Eddie! . . . Eddie! . . ." the chanting continued.

The game turned into one of the most unique in the annals of hockey, for the home town fans were cheering for the visiting goaltender. Although he was competing against their own team, stopping the shots of their own players, they

"Eddie! Eddie! Eddie!" the Ranger fans chanted, though their favorite goalie was now wearing the red uniform of the enemy.

cheered and applauded every time he made a save.

Did he win the game against his former team?

The final score was 6-4 in favor of the visiting Detroit Red Wings, whose goal had been guarded by their new keeper, Eddie Giacomin. He had blocked 38 shots, some of them in a spectacular way, and allowed only 4 goals. The crowd renewed their cheering as he skated off the ice.

Ironically, as a youth Eddie Giacomin had dreamed of

playing for Detroit, to him the finest team in hockey. He had once attended a junior tryout, hoping to be signed to play on one of Detroit's farm clubs.

But Giacomin had been discouraged by Detroit officials.

"Forget about playing goalie, son," one of them had said. "You just aren't good enough to play junior hockey."

[16]

The Golden Jet

THERE ARE CERTAIN names that will always ring out in hockey, years from now just as prominently as they do today. Maurice "Rocket" Richard, Gordie Howe, Bobby Orr, Howie Morenz, Jean Beliveau, Bobby "The Golden Jet" Hull.

These stars in one of the roughest games of all are special athletes. They will not accept defeat. Nothing seems to stop them, no injury or illness or personal setback. They come back again and again, hammering just as tenaciously as ever, until they triumph.

Yes, they feel pain, but they do not acknowledge it. Allowing pain to affect their play would be to allow pain to win, something they cannot do. For *they* must win.

So they play on in spite of injury until they do win. They know that injury is a part of the job, and so they accept it as an opponent to be fought down.

Occasionally, though, this philosophy is tested to near the breaking point. It happened once during the playoffs between Bobby Hull's Chicago Black Hawks and the tough Detroit Red Wings in 1963.

Hull had been an inspiration in the first game between the

Bobby Hull (left) raises his stick in triumph after tying the NHL scoring record of 50 goals in one season. Only Richard, Geoffrion, and Hull himself had done it before.

battling teams, scoring two goals and skating brilliantly to lead the Hawks to victory. His thirty miles per hour skating speed and his wicked slap shots were well known in the league and both were being used in the best-of-seven series of games.

The second game was going Chicago's way, then it happened. Hull was attempting to poke check the puck away from a Red Wing. He stabbed and stabbed and finally swept the puck up on his stick. Turning quickly, he moved to pass the puck to a teammate.

But at that instant the Detroit player also whirled around in an attempt to regain possession of the puck. Both players were turning quickly toward each other. The Detroit player's stick end was high and coming hard.

It smashed directly into Bobby Hull's face.

Crack!

Fans throughout the arena winced as they heard the sound of breaking bone. Hull sagged to his knees in pain, blood pouring from his misshapen nose to pool on the ice. The injury wasn't intentional, it was just one of those happenings in the high-speed, rough game of hockey.

Officials are permitted to stop the seldom-stopped game of hockey if a serious injury is apparent on the ice. Otherwise, even though he might be hurt, the flow of play continues until a player can make his own way to the bench for a substitution.

With one look at Hull, the referee blew his whistle, stopping the game and allowing the Hawks' trainer to come from the bench. The trainer and other teammates helped The Golden Jet off the ice and into the dressing room where the team doctor examined him. It didn't take but a few seconds.

"Get him to the hospital!" snapped the doctor.

It was a tough break for Hull and for Chicago. Hull was a superstar, the spark plug of the team, the player who made things happen on the ice. It seemed obvious to everyone who had seen the accident that Bobby Hull was out for the remainder of the playoffs. Players can often come back after a few days with a broken nose, but Hull's face had been smashed by the hard stick end. His nose wasn't just broken, it was a misshapen blob with a shattered bone inside.

Hull spent the night in the hospital after surgery reshaped

his nose, piecing together the parts into a reasonable, though badly swollen, facsimile of the original. Meanwhile, his eyes were blackening and swelling nearly shut. The next morning he went home to recuperate, not certain himself how he was feeling. Yes, he would recover, but his entire face was one great burning pain.

But he had to get home in order to watch the remaining games of the playoffs on television.

The Black Hawks lost the game that night.

Immediately Hull went to his telephone. He placed a call to the team doctor. "I'm flying to Detroit for the next game," he stated.

"You can't do that, Bobby," argued the doctor. "I won't permit it."

"I'm going," said Hull.

So the injured Golden Jet flew to Detroit and played in all the remaining games of the series. His face was a puffy mass of purple swelling causing him intense and constant pain. His eyes were blackened and nearly closed and a huge bandage covered the worst break in his nose, but he played brilliantly.

Can you imagine the pain he would have felt if a puck or stick hit him in the face? Perhaps Hull imagined it through the pain he was feeling. But probably he didn't.

He scored at least one goal in each of the last three games. In the sixth game, though he had only partial vision and was playing in severe pain, Bobby Hull scored a hat trick!

[17   ]

The Rocket's Goals

SOME PLAYERS, especially defensemen, go an entire season without scoring a goal. A modern hockey goal is difficult to score.

Not, perhaps, as difficult as a goal attempted by a forward who fired a hard shot at the net during an earlier-day hockey game. The puck in those days was for some reason made up of two halves that had been cemented together.

When this player hit the puck it split apart in two sections and, as luck would have it, one part went into the corner of the rink but the other one skimmed into the goal.

The referee calmly looked at the rule book, then, in spite of half the players shouting "Goal!" and the other half shouting "No goal!", he disallowed the score. "The hockey puck, according to the rule book, must be one inch thick. That object in the goal is only one-half-inch thick. Thus it is not legal, thus it was not a legal goal."

But then as now, a hockey goal is a tough score. Hockey is a game that pits thunder against lightning, the immovable object against the irresistible force. When a goal is scored,

100

something has gone wrong but something else has gone right. A hockey goal is a thrilling paradox.

In the 1860s the hockey puck was a round ball and not the flattened disc it is today. But during a game at Montreal's Victoria Skating Rink, the ball was fired over the boards several times with such force that it shattered a number of arena windows. After several hundred dollars worth of damage, the manager of the rink was at the end of his patience.

When the next ball was tossed out to continue the game, he grabbed it. Taking a sharp knife, he cut off the top and bottom, making the ball into a flattened disc. This would cut down on the broken windows, he was sure. The game then continued and the players liked the new puck so well that it has remained that shape ever since.

That inch-thick ounce of rubber was the plaything of Maurice Richard. Richard could make a puck dance, darting in and out and around and through opponents until he fired it or flicked it past the frustrated goaltender. The Montreal Canadiens have always been a top team and Richard was one of the star players on that team.

But even the Rocket will remember forever the game with the Toronto Maple Leafs on March 23, 1944, and what the puck did for him that night. Perhaps it was on that night that fans realized what might happen in the future, for this was only the second year in the league for Richard.

Coach Dick Irvin had young Richard playing on the famous "Punch Line." A "line" in hockey is made up of a center and two wings, or three players. There are normally three lines on a hockey team. Each line goes into the game together, so individual line players become accustomed to

Maurice Richard could make the puck dance. Here he battles with almost the entire Boston Bruins team during 1956 action.

playing together. Fans can see that a team is in trouble when the coach begins to shift around the players from line to line, trying new combinations, seeking the best goal-scoring group.

The Punch Line was not tampered with, for it was one of the best scoring lines in hockey. Elmer Lach was at center,

Toe Blake was at left wing, and Richard was at right wing. Because the Punch Line was such a high-scoring combination, other teams dreaded to see them leap over the wall and skate onto the ice together.

Big Bob Davidson, a hard-checking forward, had been assigned to see that Richard didn't score during the playoffs with the Leafs that year. Whenever Richard and his linemates would come on, so would Davidson. In the first game Davidson shadowed Richard closely, bumping him and shoving him every time Richard received the puck. The Rocket did not score a single goal.

The second game started in much the same way. Davidson hounded Richard and through the entire first period the star Canadien player did not get a shot at the goal. In the second period, though, Maurice Richard came back with a *roar*.

Defenseman Mike McMahon grabbed the puck in the Montreal zone and shot it up the ice to Elmer Lach. Lach glanced over and saw that Richard was moving in on the goal. He had skated ahead of Davidson with one of the lightning-fast moves he was famous for. Lach shot a perfect pass across the ice to the Rocket's stick and Richard moved in on Toronto goalie Mike Bibeault. He faked one way and shot the other. Bibeault lunged, but it was too late. The puck skimmed past his outstretched hand.

Score!

The goal drought of Richard had been broken. He skated away with his stick held high as the referee prepared to begin the game anew with a face-off at center ice.

Less than 20 seconds later, Lach and Blake set up a play, fired the puck to Richard, and again he shot it past Bibeault.

Another score! The game stood at Montreal 2, Toronto 0.

Quickly Toronto fought back. While Davidson attempted to hold Richard in check, Reg Hamilton made a goal for the Leafs. The score was 2-1.

Near the end of the second period Lach and Blake once again set up Richard and he streaked in on Bibeault. With a fake one way, he fired the puck past the goalie. Richard had earned a rare *playoff* hat trick and all three goals had come in one period. It suddenly began to look like a runaway for Montreal, and the fans thundered their approval. The score going into the third period was 3-1. The Canadiens charged onto the ice to finish off the Leafs.

One minute into the final period the Punch Line clicked again. The puck skimmed from Lach to Blake to Richard, and into the goal. The score was 4-1, and all four goals had been scored by Rocket Richard. Midway in the same period it happened again. The Punch Line skated up the ice, passing the puck back and forth as desperate defensemen tried to sweep it away. Almost quicker than the eye could follow it was flicked across to Richard and he flipped it over the stick of Bibeault into the net.

Montreal fans erupted in a storm of applause. Not only was their team winning easily, but they had seen history made. It was a record then and it has remained a record to this day in hockey. No other player has ever scored five goals in a single Stanley Cup playoff game. The Canadiens won the game 5-1, and all five goals were Maurice Richard's.

It is customary in hockey for an expert, usually a knowledgable journalist covering the game, to select three "stars" from each game. These three players skate onto the ice after the game for an extra cheer. They can come from the beaten team or the winning team. They are called "Star Number

One," "Star Number Two," and "Star Number Three." The announcement was made:

> Star Number Three was Maurice Richard.
> Star Number Two was Maurice Richard.
> Star Number One was, yes, Maurice Richard.

And that, too, has never happened again.

[18]

Eddie Shore and Ace Bailey

EDWARD WILLIAM SHORE of Fort Qu'Appelle, Saskatchewan, known as "Eddie" or, to sportswriters, the "Edmonton Express," was one of the most feared defensemen in hockey. Often compared to Bobby Orr as one of the two best defensemen in the history of the sport, Shore's fame came from his tough-as-nails outlook.

Like Orr, Shore played for Boston, and Kyle Crichton wrote in *Collier's* magazine why Eddie drew more fans to the ice rinks than any other player.

"What makes him that way is the hope, entertained by spectators in all cities but Boston," wrote Crichton, "that he will some night be severely killed."

Shore played tough when the game of hockey was tougher than it is today. He played with bruises, cuts, aches and pains, and broken bones. Once he finished a game in spite of a broken nose, three cracked ribs, two black eyes, and a brain concussion. Yes, then he went in for treatment, but he was back on the ice the *very next night*. He antagonized players on the other team regardless of their size or fighting ability. To him they were the enemy, *all* of them. Shore knew that he would have to pay with pain for his playing style, and he did, but he always tried to give as much as he had to take.

He was a hard, strictly disciplined player who was selected Most Valuable Player four times and served on All-Star teams seven times during his stormy career. He helped to win two Stanley Cups. He was a hockey player who seldom looked back, but one time Eddie Shore did look back and admit he had been wrong.

It began during a game between Boston and the Toronto Maple Leafs in the Boston Garden. It was December 12, 1933.

The game was hard fought through most of the first period and though they were only leading by one goal, the Leafs were outplaying the Boston team. Frustrated Boston players were growing angrier and angrier and finally a fight flared on the ice. The result was that two Toronto players, Andy Blair and Hap Day, were sent to the penalty box. What a break for Boston!

The Leafs' penalty-killing unit roared onto the ice. One of the defensemen was an ace penalty killer, one of the best in the league. His name was Irvin "Ace" Bailey. Bailey was noted for his superb stickhandling. He could carry the puck through an entire team, leaving them befuddled and in confusion.

The puck was passed to Bailey and he went into his act, zigging and zagging this way and that, carrying the puck around and through the Boston team, eating up second after second of the two-minute penalties being served by his teammates. The Boston team chased him in anger, but he eluded them. Finally the referee called for another face-off, ruling that Bailey was not advancing the puck according to the rules.

Again Bailey controlled the puck for a time before shooting it deep into the Boston zone. Instantly defenseman Eddie Shore picked it up and started one of his great charges up the ice. But King Clancy of the Toronto team swept in and, with what was later called an illegal tap to the skates, sent Shore sprawling on the ice. Clancy controlled the puck and started back for the Boston goal.

Eddie Shore, meanwhile, was sagging on the ice, regaining his senses from the hard fall. Finally he staggered to his skates. Some say he was hoping for a penalty to be called. He was known as one of the great actors in the league. Baz O'Meara wrote in the *Montreal Star* that Shore "could do a dying-swan act that would have aroused the envy of Margot Fonteyn."

But Shore wasn't acting. He was blistering mad. Spotting Bailey at center ice, bent over his stick and looking the other way, Eddie dug in and started toward the Leaf. Maybe he thought Bailey was King Clancy, or maybe Eddie just saw an enemy uniform.

The Edmonton Express was up to full speed before he hit Bailey from behind with his shoulder. Bailey flipped high into the air and came down on his head with a sickening thud heard throughout the arena. Then he seemed to go limp, his neck at an odd angle and his leg twitching.

A few in the arena cheered, but most of the fans could see that Bailey had been seriously injured. Meanwhile, Leaf Red Horner hit Eddie Shore, knocking him to the ice, and there he lay, a red halo of blood oozing from a bad gash in his head. Quickly action stopped and players and officials rushed to the two injured men.

Bailey was taken to a hospital where emergency surgery kept him alive. Then another massive blood clot formed on his brain, and again surgery was required. His life was hanging by a thread and for many weeks the daily reports in the newspapers were pessimistic.

Recovered, Eddie Shore continued to play hockey for Boston. The word finally came on Ace Bailey. He would recover, but he would never play hockey again. The star player was out of the game forever.

On February 14, 1934, the Toronto Maple Leafs played a benefit game for Ace Bailey. To be sure to attract fans, the opponents were to be the All-Star players from the other teams in the National Hockey League. Included on any All-Star team had to be the great defenseman, Eddie Shore, though many fans had demanded that he be blacklisted from hockey forever.

Eddie Shore and Ace Bailey side by side at the benefit game for Bailey after his release from the hospital. League officials stand by, and famous announcer Foster Hewitt is at the microphone.

Boos thundered down from the stands as the players lined up for introductions, for Eddie Shore was in the line. At center ice stood a pale and wan Ace Bailey, just released from the hospital. Eddie Shore looked across at his former enemy and as the boos and catcalls continued to roll down over the ice, he skated across and put out his hand.

For only an instant Bailey looked, then he grasped the hand of Eddie Shore and the two men embraced.

A great cheer suddenly came from the fans. If Ace could forgive Eddie, so could they. They continued to cheer as Shore played his usual hard-checking game that night.

The next morning writer Elmer Ferguson summed it up in the *Montreal Herald*. "It was a generous, fine and sporting episode in a sporting city's history."

As it truly was.

Penalties, and One That Was Asked For

IT WAS ONE of the roughest hockey games ever played. The players were beaten and bruised, the ice was stained with blood, broken sticks were littered about, and near the end of the game both Ottawa and Kenora—early-day pro hockey teams—were at the end of their endurance.

One of the Kenora forwards poke-checked the puck from an Ottawa player, then started around his own goal to set up a play. Quickly he was tripped by another Ottawa player. He hit the ice hard and skidded, bleeding and stunned, across his own goal crease, blocking the goal.

He tried to rise but sagged back to the ice in a near unconscious state.

Usually a referee will blow the game to a stop when a player is injured, but this referee raised his arm for a *penalty*. When play stopped he assessed the injured player a five-minute stay in the penalty box for delaying the game and obstructing his own goal.

Hockey has never been a game for the faint-hearted or the

Hockey has never been a game for the faint-hearted or the weak in spirit. Boldness counts in hockey.

weak in spirit. Boldness counts in hockey and crybabies don't last long. Many players are proud of the time they spend in the penalty box, figuring that although their own team must play short-handed during these periods of time, they have gained by the fear they have put into the opposing team.

Of course even referees make mistakes. Ching Johnson, a

Hall of Famer who played magnificent defense in pro hockey for eleven years and then played on in the minor leagues until he was forty-six years old, finally turned to refereeing. At age fifty he was calling a game between the Washington Lions and the New York Rovers when one of the Washington players suddenly broke away from the action and started for the New York goal all alone.

Such a play many times results in an almost certain goal, and such a play is always like waving a red flag at a hockey defenseman.

Like an old war horse reacting almost instinctively, referee Johnson skated quickly across the ice and flattened the amazed player with a hard body check.

"I can't explain it," Johnson said later. "Here was a guy skating for the goal and I had to stop him. The old habit was too deep within me. I forgot where I was and what I was doing."

Not that *any* player ever *asks* a referee to call a penalty against him. Except for another Hall of Famer, "King" Clancy, that is.

Clancy was the Toronto Maple Leaf player who also became a noted hockey referee after he ended his playing days. He was a player who one night in Boston in the 1930s finally became angry at a fan. The fan in the seats near the ice had been on him since the game started, hurling insults every time Clancy skated by. Finally King could stand no more. He skated up to the boards and snapped, "You think you're pretty tough, don't you? Just stick around after the game and we'll see how tough you really are!"

The fan smiled in delight as Clancy skated away. Quickly

King Clancy, who eventually became a fine referee, had a chance to become the World Heavyweight Champion and wisely rejected the "opportunity."

another player skated over to the still-boiling Clancy.

"Hey, you'll be champion of the world if you handle that guy, King. Don't you recognize him?"

Clancy looked again and decided to pass up the chance to "see how tough" the fan was that night. For the fan who had been provoking him all evening was none other than the World Heavyweight Champion, Jack Sharkey.

It was during an earlier-day hockey game that Clancy had his unusual penalty incident. In those days teams carried very few substitutes. Hockey was a 60-minute game for most of the players. Substituting every few seconds was unheard of in those days, though it is common in modern hockey.

King Clancy had played the entire game, since the team's only substitute defenseman had been too ill to play that night. By the middle of the third period, he was completely worn out. He could barely lift his stick, let alone skate quickly back and forth on the ice.

Finally he could take no more. He was sagging with fatigue. He waved across the ice to his bench, indicating that he needed a rest. There was a substitute forward on the bench, and Clancy figured that he could come in as a defenseman for at least a few minutes, to give him a breather.

"My lungs were bursting and my arms and legs were numb with fatigue," said Clancy, who led the Leafs to a Stanley Cup win in his first year on the team. "I could hardly stand."

No, the coach shook his head. Then he indicated with a wave that Clancy should remain in the game.

But King Clancy knew that he was through, unless he had a rest. So he made up his mind. The next enemy player that skated by became his target. Clancy simply reached out with his stick, making no attempt at all to hide his move. He jammed the stick between the player's legs and cleanly tripped him, sending him sprawling on the ice.

Instantly the referee's arm shot up and the whistle blew. Clancy was sent to the penalty box for two minutes for the tripping infraction . . . and for a needed and well-deserved two-minute rest.

[20]

Hockey Has Some Nice Guys, Too

HOCKEY PLAYERS will do anything to get a goal, or so it is said. They have a reputation for trampling over anybody to get the puck in the net.

This is not always true.

Gump Worsley was playing goalie for the New York Rangers one night against the vaunted Detroit Red Wings. With the Wings was a player who had a reputation as a mean man for reasons never quite clear. Although this player had hurt other players on the ice over the years, it was generally conceded that like an honorable gunfighter from the Old West, he had never hurt anybody he didn't think deserved it.

He was also one of the finest players in the history of hockey, the great Gordie Howe.

When goaltenders saw Howe streaking in they would wince and be ready to be hit by a blistering slap shot. Howe's shot was always hard and usually on target. This night he wound up and let fly at 120 miles per hour a shot at Worsley. At the last instant Gump flopped on his belly and blocked the shot with his body.

One of the all-time great goalies in the history of hockey, Lorne "Gump" Worsley, turns away a shot fired by a Detroit Red Wing.

Stunned by the force of the puck hitting him, there was no way Worsley could contain the rebound. The puck skipped off him to come to rest inches from his unprotected, maskless face. What was worse, much worse, for Worsley, the puck had also come to a rest directly on the stick of the same Gordie Howe. Howe saw the puck and the situation of Gump Worsley. He had a certain goal if he wanted to take it.

"If he wanted to he could have just snapped his wrists and put the puck, and my head, into the goal," Worsley said later. Fans in the stands could see that a quick shot by Howe would result in a goal, but also in almost certain injury to the goalie. Meanwhile, other players were converging on the scene of action and in seconds Worsley was going to have to contend with not only the puck but with razor-sharp skates next to his nose.

118

Without hesitation, Howe leaned over and shoved the puck under the helpless goalie. Quickly Worsley smothered it and the whistle blew for a face-off.

As Worsley scrambled to his feet, he looked up at Gordie Howe. "Thanks, Bud, but you'll get it next time."

Howe, who had without doubt saved Worsley from a serious injury, merely looked back with a half-smile on his face, then, saying nothing, he skated away.

He knew he would get another shot at Worsley, and it wouldn't be a cheap shot.

In a game between the St. Louis Blues and the Chicago Black Hawks, the heart of hockey players surfaced again. The other player noted for his fast slap shot, Bobby Hull, was in this game. So were Stan Mikita and other fine players from both teams.

The game was a tough one, holding the fans on the edges of their seats. The checking had been hard but clean. It was obvious that each team respected the other and that both teams expected to win.

Suddenly, in the third period of the game, the Black Hawks' Stan Mikita skated free in a clean breakaway. Instantly he headed toward the Blues' goal, stickhandling the puck one way and then the other to confuse goalie Ernie Wakely. He didn't want Wakely to know exactly which way the shot would be coming from.

In hockey, in a situation like this, the defense will generally go to almost any extreme, even incur a penalty, to stop a breakaway player. Defenseman Andre Dupont, closing from the rear, did a fine job of harrying Mikita, and Stan's hurried shot was bounced away by Wakely. A good chance for a goal had been turned into just another exciting shot.

But the play wasn't over. Far from it, and what happened next proved that hockey players, though tough, are sportsmen.

Dupont, worrying more about harassing Mikita than about himself, sprawled on the ice just as the shot was being taken. His speed was high and he skidded across the ice and into the goal net behind his goalie. As he passed the goal posts his head struck with a loud ring that could be heard far up in the stands back of the goal.

In the nets, he lay unmoving.

Wakely took one look and waved for help from the Blues' bench. Meanwhile, it was as if somebody had frozen the action on the ice. With the sound of Dupont's head striking the steel post, every other player stopped and turned. They knew the Blues' defenseman had been badly hurt.

Quickly Lloyd Gilmour, the referee, blew his whistle to stop play officially, then he skated to the goal. Mikita had already spun about on his skates and moved to help the fallen player. He dropped down alongside the injured defenseman.

The Blues' Bob Plager hurried down to the other end of the rink for a stretcher and at the same time Mikita skated around the net to bang with his stick on the exit leading to the visitor's dressing room. Normally closed from the other side during the games, Mikita knew that the exit would be the quickest way to get Dupont off the ice and to medical help.

The trainers from both teams tried to hurry to the scene, slipping and sliding across the ice. Finally the Blues' trainer, Tom Woodcock, was almost bodily picked up by Blues players Jerry Korab and Frank St. Marseille and skidded the last

120

couple dozen feet. Two other players lifted Chicago trainer Skip Thayer to the goal in case he could help.

When Coach Al Arbour stepped onto the ice, referee Gilmour and linesman Neil Armstrong grabbed him and steered him to the fallen Blues defenseman. Meanwhile, players from both teams skated around, passing the goal to check and offer help, then skating on to give the trainers room to work. Dr. J.G. Probstein, the Blues' physician, stepped gingerly on the ice and instantly Blues Bob Plager and Black Hawk Bobby Hull took his arms and helped him to the goal where Dupont lay injured. Plager and Hull were enemies, but not at that moment.

After a quick examination, the doctor ordered Dupont to the hospital. He was carried out through the exit Mikita had had the foresight to have opened. Then two more players guided the doctor off the ice. The two trainers thanked each other as players gathered momentarily to discuss the accident.

Then the whistle blew for a face-off to continue the game.

In only a few seconds Bob Plager checked Bobby Hull hard into the boards and a moment later Hull did the same to Plager. Two players who had stood side by side waiting to help Dupont erupted into a battle on the ice. The tough game was back on and both teams still wanted to win.

But in that moment of need, everybody had worked together to help a fallen player. The symbols on the uniforms had meant nothing.

[21]
Hull's 51st Goal

THERE WAS A time in the career of the great Bobby Hull when he began receiving gifts through the mail. It is perhaps not that unusual for a star athlete to receive gifts from his fans, but Hull's gifts were unusual.

They were coming in batches of fifty-one.

Most of the gifts came from Chicago, home of Hull's Black Hawks. They included fifty-one cans of soup, fifty-one jars of jam, and fifty-one Kennedy half dollars. One fan sent him fifty-one boxes of cereal. A warehouse in Chicago offered him free space to store his gifts . . . but for just fifty-one days.

On March 2, 1966, Bobby Hull had scored his 50th goal. Only the great Maurice Richard and his teammate, Boom Boom Geoffrion, both of the Montreal Canadiens, had managed that many goals in one season before. Hull, himself, had accomplished the feat once before, four years earlier, but he had done it during the final game of the season, so there was no chance to break the record and stand alone.

On that night in 1966 there remained 13 games before the season was over. Hull had thirteen more games in which to break a long-standing hockey record and become the only player in history to score 51 goals in a season. Among other places in the record book of the National Hockey League, Bobby Hull's name is still listed first under the section "Most Games Scoring Three or More Goals." Hull scored a hat trick in 28 games during his career. He had four different 4-goal games. There seemed little doubt that this ace shooter would score at least one more goal in thirteen games to become the all-time leader in goals scored in a single season. (The Goals Scored in a Season figures are higher today because many more games are now played in a single season.)

But suddenly Hull, and Chicago, slipped into a scoring slump. The Hawks began to lose as the pressure for Hull's number 51 increased. Fans became more and more restive, sure that the team was feeling the pressure, and losing games because of it.

Newspapers and magazines headlined the question: WHEN WILL HULL GET HIS 51ST GOAL?

Two games immediately following Hull's 50th goal were shutouts against Chicago, an unbelievable occurrence for a team with shooting stars like Hull, Stan Mikita, Kenny Wharram, Doug Mohns, and other fine players. Chicago players were getting irritated with each other and the pressure seemed to increase with each day.

After a game with the New York Rangers (Chicago was shut out) a local paper headlined: WILL ANY HAWK SCORE? Players were getting desperate, the press was getting desperate, and fans were getting desperate. Everyone wanted that goal, especially Hull, but it just wouldn't come.

Finally, on March 12, 1966, the Black Hawks lined up for another game with the Rangers. But things seemed to be going no better than before. For two long periods, though the Hawks and Hull himself were getting shots at the goal, there was no Chicago score. The team appeared to be headed for still another shutout.

Suddenly Hull grabbed the puck. He had already been on the move toward the Ranger goal so his speed was high. Sensing what was about to happen, the fans began one long drawn-out cheer as Hull streaked down the ice.

Goalie Cesare Maniago moved out away from the crease to cut down on the angle of the shot he was sure was coming. Hull's slap shots were known to be extremely fast, and Maniago wanted to be ready. But at the last instant Hull, instead of shooting for the goal himself, saw that Black Hawk Chico Maki was in a better position for a shot. Hull flicked the puck across the ice to Maki and with Maniago out of position, Maki skidded it into the goal.

The Hawks had finally scored!

Though it hadn't been the sought-after 51st goal of Hull, it was a goal and that seemed to lift the pressure from the Black Hawks. They began to play with their old assurance, with the fluid looseness of a champion, as they had played all season long.

In the third period Lou Angotti of the Hawks stole the puck from a Ranger then kicked it over to Hull with his skate. Hull was just crossing the Rangers' blue line. Meanwhile, to Hull's right, Eric Nesterenko cut across in front of Cesare Maniago, partially screening Hull from the Rangers' goaltender. Maniago tried to move out to cut down the angle, but at that instant Hull let go with his slap shot. The puck streaked low across the ice, with every eye in the stadium following its flight.

Maniago made a desperate, last-instant try to block the

124

Bobby Hull, the great Chicago Black Hawk, stands amid a shower of hats and accepts the cheers of Chicago fans for his record-breaking 51st goal in one season.

shot, but Nesterenko turned and skillfully lifted the blade of the goalie's stick. Maniago missed. The puck slammed into the Rangers' goal. As it did, Hull skimmed past the goal crease, stick high in the air.

Instantly the grandstands erupted in a tremendous roar. It was a new record!

The red light flashed on to confirm the goal as the fans continued their long explosion. Bells clanged and whistles blew. Debris showered the ice. Hats skimmed down to slide across the ice around Hull. Programs filled the air like confetti, newspapers and hotdog wrappers flew down from the stands in tribute to the man who had just broken the scoring record. In the grandstands Bobby Hull's wife was crying in triumph and relief. Hull skated down to the end of the rink to lean over the boards and kiss her. Again the crowd exploded in applause.

Then he skated to one of the hats, put it on at a jaunty angle and skated around the rink to renewed cheers.

For many long minutes the game was delayed as the standing ovation continued. Hull would go to the bench and then return to the ice as the roar increased. There he would wave and smile. Again and again he was called back to the ice, thankful that he had broken the record at his own home rink before his own loyal fans.

22

The Least Expensive Hero in Hockey History

BY SOME STROKE of luck which nobody can yet figure out, the struggling 1938 Chicago Black Hawks found themselves in the Stanley Cup finals against the powerful Toronto Maple Leafs. It was a foregone conclusion that the Leafs would win. Chicago had only won the famous Cup once in the forty-one years of its existence. What was worse, Chicago was playing some *American* players instead of Canadians, unheard of in pro hockey in the pre-World War II days. The Leafs had crushed their opponents all year long, while the Hawks had won only *fourteen* games the *entire season*.

The Hawks had come back to play well in the playoffs, but the odds were that the Maple Leafs would overwhelm the Chicago team in four easy games.

Some Toronto fans were even betting that the Black Hawks wouldn't bother to show up for the games. Instead, insisted these fans, the Hawks would just mail in a string of 0's to be attached to whatever scores the Toronto team wanted to give themselves.

The Black Hawks did show up for the game at the Maple

Leaf Gardens, but that very evening the final blow seemed to fall on the Chicagoans. The Hawk goaltender, Mike Karakas, was having great difficulty putting on a skate over a foot that was swollen and black. A doctor was called and the diagnosis was made. The toe that had been bothering Karakas since the last practice session was broken. He would not be able to play that night.

Desperately Chicago coach Bill Stewart began to look for a replacement goalie. There were rules about these matters. It was not that easy to bring in a new player not already on your roster. The other team had something to say about that, according to the regulations. But time was running out. Stewart knew that beggars couldn't be choosers, but he didn't want the playoffs to be a complete washout, as they would be if he tried to use a regular Chicago player as goalie. Still, every goalie available around the Gardens was rejected by the Toronto Maple Leafs' brass.

Finally Stewart stumbled across Alfie Moore. Not that interested in the Cup finals, Moore was down the street in a bar having a beer.

Who was Alfie Moore? That's what the Chicago team was asking. In fact, the fans were asking it too. Nobody had ever heard of him. Moore was a minor league goalie with an obscure reputation who had, until then, led a hockey career that was distinguished by its obscurity. Not because Alfie wanted it that way, but because that was the way he played goalie.

He was considered so inept, in fact, that Toronto agreed he could be used in the Hawks' net.

It is said that we all get at least one real chance for the gold ring. One shot at hitting it big. Opportunity knocks on every

Alfie Moore heard opportunity knocking and played the game of his life for the Chicago Black Hawks during their Stanley Cup opener with Toronto. He is seen here in an Americans' uniform with the famous Turk Broda of Toronto.

door sooner or later. Whether or not we hear it is another matter. Alfie Moore heard it loud and clear. He didn't even bother to discuss pay with Stewart, he was so anxious to play.

The very first shot of the game, blasted at Moore by Toronto's Gordie Drillon, swished past Alfie into the net. He never even saw it coming, and Chicago settled back for what they thought was going to be a long, *long* night.

Then Alfie settled down.

He played hockey with a skill called up from a reserve nobody ever thought he had. He blocked shot after shot from every angle, throwing himself across the crease, stretching his body desperately, uncaring where the hard puck hit him. It was a magnificent exhibition of goaltending and it inspired the Chicago Black Hawks to greater and greater efforts at the Toronto goal.

The obscure Moore allowed only that one goal in the entire game. It was the best, and last, such game he ever played. But he went out in a blaze of glory on his teammates' shoulders. For when the final buzzer sounded, the unbelieving Toronto fans realized that Chicago had won by a score of 3-1.

Back in the dressing room after the game, coach Stewart approached Alfie Moore.

"Great game, Alfie. Now how much do we owe you?"

Battered and bruised, Moore thought quickly. He knew he would never have another chance like this. He would set the figure at the highest possible point, as high as he thought the Chicago coach would go. But no higher. He didn't want to look too greedy and lose everything. He made up his mind and just blurted out the stunning figure.

"How about . . . one hundred and . . . and fifty dollars," said Alfie Moore with a choke in his throat.

Stewart *was* stunned. This obscure goalie, with supreme effort, had turned the Hawks around. They had won that critical first game. Stewart knew that Moore had used every single ounce of what he had and that it probably would never happen again. He knew that the Hawks could not go on without their regular goalie, Karakas.

Alfie Moore knew it, too.

Reaching into his wallet, the coach drew out three hundred dollars and handed it to the happy substitute.

With Karakas back in the nets, wearing a special shoe to protect his foot, the Hawks went on to win the Stanley Cup that year. Oddly, they did not get physical possession of the Cup until later. League president Frank Calder had been so certain that a ragtag American team could never win the coveted Cup that he had ordered it sent on to Toronto even before the series started. Nobody remembered to bring it to Chicago until it was too late.

Alfie Moore, the goalie who so inspired the team that they beat the mighty Maple Leafs, drifted back into obscurity with a final tribute, a gold watch presented to him by the Black Hawks. But for one bright, shining moment, he was hockey's great hero. For this, he earned a place in the lore of the rugged sport.

23

Out of the Dressing Room and into the Penalty Box

STAN MIKITA, another of the great players in the history of hockey, once came back from the dressing room to serve out a penalty and help win a game he thought was over. The game was played the night of March 26, 1961, in Chicago Stadium. Playing against Mikita's Black Hawks were the feared Montreal Canadiens, a team that had won the Stanley Cup the previous *five years*.

It was the third game of the first-round playoffs for the Cup. The first game had been won by the Canadiens, the second by the Black Hawks. Both games had been played in Montreal. Back on home ice, the Hawks felt they had a definite advantage going into the third game in the best-of-seven series.

The problem really started in the penalty box. None of the Canadien players on that team, including such greats as Boom Boom Geoffrion, Dickie Moore, and Jean Beliveau, were known to take much shoving around. Neither was Black Hawk Mikita, for that matter. The hard-checking game was nearly over, with the Hawks leading by a score of 1-

0, when Mikita and Bill Hicke tangled on the ice. Unpleasant words were spoken and finally the two dropped their gloves and began to punch at each other.

Quickly they were separated and sent to the penalty box for two minutes each. The trouble was, there was only a minute left to play in the game. Neither player thought he would get a chance to play again that night.

This became even more obvious when as they seated themselves to watch the end of the game, Hicke couldn't resist one last uncomplimentary remark at Mikita. Mikita, a player never known to take anything fron an enemy, answered back and the fight was on again. Fists were flying with even more fury than they had been out on the ice. Officials in the box ducked out of the way and fans screamed as the two battled.

It took linesmen several minutes to pull the two players apart, then referee Dalt McArthur calmly skated in to assess what he considered to be proper punishment for the fight in the box. He was very strict.

Both Hicke and Mikita received an additional five minutes for fighting plus ten more minutes for misconduct. Fifteen minutes on top of the two they had received for the original fight. Plainly, the game was over for them.

Looking at the time remaining and anxious to get the two out of the box and separated for good, the referee said, "You guys might as well go down to the dressing room. You won't be playing any more tonight."

How wrong he was!

Mikita took the advice, though, and went downstairs to the Hawks' dressing room. He was sure the Hawks had the game won and he could get a headstart in the shower. But just as he was taking off his uniform he heard a tremendous roar com-

Stan Mikita, another of the great players of hockey and a star Black Hawk, is checked from behind by the late Tim Horton of the Toronto Maple Leafs.

ing from upstairs. It was action on the ice, he knew, but exactly what it was shouldn't have any effect on him. He was out of the game one way or the other.

A few seconds later his teammates trooped down into the dressing room. But not to undress. What had happened was that Canadien Henri Richard, younger brother of the great Maurice Richard, had scored a last-second goal against the Black Hawks. The score was tied 1-1.

The game was going into sudden-death overtime.

Coach Rudy Pilous hurried up to Mikita. "You'd better get dressed again," he ordered. "We might need you."

So Stan Mikita, with 16 minutes left to serve of his third period penalty, put on his uniform and joined his team as they skated out onto the ice for the first overtime period. He skated directly to the penalty box, grinning at referee Mc-Arthur as he passed.

Mikita did play again in the game, for as his penalty expired near the end of the first overtime period the score was still tied 1-1.

At the end of the second overtime period it was *still* 1-1 and Mikita was back at his position. Both teams had several opportunities to score, but last-second defensive maneuvers by inspired goaltenders kept the game going.

In the third overtime period referee McArthur called a penalty against the Canadiens. The penalty call later cost him a punch in the nose by irate Canadiens' coach Toe Blake, who was fined $2,000 by the league for the blow.

Why was Blake so irritated? The penalty meant that Montreal had to skate short-handed for two long minutes. That gave Chicago the break they had been waiting for. They set up their power play, confident that they could score and end the long game.

Mikita was playing right point. He shot in to Murray Balfour in front of the net, and Balfour tipped the puck into the Canadiens' goal to win the game. Mikita, who had earlier been sent out of the game for good, had set up the score with the winning assist.

What's more, the Hawks continued on to eliminate the Canadiens that year, then beat Detroit in 6 games to win the coveted Stanley Cup.

24

Orr!

THOUGH HE WAS a tough fighter with a short fuse early in his career, Bobby Orr began to feel that sitting out penalties was foolish when you could be on the ice scoring.

With that attitude, he became consistent highest scoring defenseman in hockey, with a blistering slap shot that skimmed past a goalkeeper before he even saw it coming. Orr could shoot from any angle and any position.

A scorer first and a fighter second, that was what Bobby Orr was in hockey. Some say he was a pure hockey machine, with no bad moves at all. Everything he did on the ice was perfect. One player grinned at a black eye Orr received in a fight on the ice and said, "That shiner was the first real indication I'd had the guy was *human*."

Once in early 1977 after a many-week layoff because of his bad knees, Bobby Orr skated into a game. His *very first* shot on goal was a *score*. One opposing coach half-jokingly suggested that the National Hockey League make a new rule—against Orr ever playing hockey again.

The great Gordie Howe was once asked what he thought

Bobby Orr's best moves were. "Just putting on his skates," answered Howe.

Still, when Orr first came to the Boston Bruins, they were far from the "Big Bad Bruins" they later became. They were the doormat of the league, in last place. The team never came close to the championship. In 1966, Orr's first year, they won only 17 of their 70 games.

But they gradually began to build, and with Orr and other stars like Phil Esposito, Ken Hodge, Johnny Bucyk, and Derek Sanderson, they started to win games. It was with a lusty desire that they finally found themselves in the Stanley Cup finals against the St. Louis Blues in 1970. The Bruins had not won the great silver trophy signifying the best team in hockey for twenty-nine long years. Boston was *ready*.

The first two games of the best-of-seven series were played in St. Louis, but even the home ice advantage didn't help the expansion Blues against the aroused Bruins. Boston won both games. On almost every goal, Orr seemed to be helping. He was everywhere on the ice, a skating dynamo and an inspiration to his team.

Back in Boston the fans were fighting for tickets. If the Bruins could win both of the upcoming games on their own home ice, they would win the Cup. Seldom was a Stanley Cup series settled in four games, but why not? The last time Boston won the Cup, they had won it in four games.

Back to Boston stormed the Bruins, ready for *action*.

In the third game the story was the same. An inspired Bruins team overpowered the Blues, outshooting them 46-21 and winning the game 4-1.

Then, at last, came the fourth game of the series. For Boston, the chips were down. If they could win this one last game, they would be the champions of all of hockey after nearly thirty years of waiting.

For the Blues, the chips were also down. There would be no more chances after this night. The game was to be televised across the United States. The Blues pulled themselves together for one final supreme effort to stop the Boston team. The Blues had seemed to be playing better and better as the series progressed. This was their last chance.

Glenn Hall, who frequently became ill before a hockey game because of the great tension of his job, was tending the Blues' goal. In the net for Boston was Gerry Cheevers. Both men were fine goaltenders.

Early in the first period of the game Boston scored and the fans began to celebrate. But wait! St. Louis charged back to rip a shot past Cheevers and the score was tied as the first period ended.

The second period had barely started when Blues' defenseman Gary Sabourin blasted a 35-foot shot past Cheevers and St. Louis was ahead. Boston fans were becoming worried. Both teams were tiring from the three previous games and this hard battle. Strength was fading. Suddenly Phil Esposito flipped a high shot over Hall's shoulder and again the score was tied. The second period ended and the players trooped wearily back to the dressing room for a needed break.

Quickly, with renewed drive, the Blues scored as the third period opened. The Bruins seemed sapped and worn out. Still they fought back. But every shot on goal was blocked by Hall and meanwhile St. Louis continued to charge the Boston goal and Cheevers. Instead of sitting back and protecting their lead, they wanted more goals.

Finally, with the Boston crowd on its feet imploring the

The fantastic horizontal shot of Bobby Orr that won the Stanley Cup for Boston in 1970. Orr could be the single greatest player in the history of hockey.

team to score, Johnny Bucyk took a pass from a teammate and slipped it past the tireless Hall. *Again* the score was tied and the crowd was alternately frantic and then sagging back quietly in their seats.

In spite of supreme efforts by both teams, regulation play ended with the score still tied. Sudden-death overtime was started. The first team to score would win.

It happened in a flash. Sanderson shot the puck into the Blues' end and Orr rushed after it. He stole it off the stick of a St. Louis player and shoved it back to Sanderson who was just skating behind the St. Louis net. Then Orr started across the slot in front of the goal. At that instant Sanderson flicked the puck back at him over the stick of a Blues defenseman.

140

No! Several St. Louis players could see what was happening. At that point, in a sudden-death overtime of what could be the last game of a Stanley Cup series, most hockey players are trained to do *anything* to stop the flow of the play.

Anything!

Almost as if in slow motion Noel Picard stretched his stick out and jammed it between the streaking Orr's skates. At the very same instant Orr was twisting his wrists for a shot back toward a narrow, unprotected corner of the St. Louis goal. Orr's feet left the ice and he finished his shot stretched out three feet above the ice.

The red light flashed on! It was a goal! The game was over. Boston had won the Stanley Cup with a fantastic, horizontal shot. Orr's teammates mobbed him, falling to the ice to roll about with him in glee, as saddened St. Louis players skated away.

Index

Abdul-Jabbar, Kareem, 53
American Hockey League, 85
Anderson, Lorne, 56
Angotti, Lou, 124
Arbour, Al, 121
Armstrong, Neil, 121

Backstrom, Ralph, 58
Bailey, Irvin "Ace," 107–110
Balfour, Murray, 136
Barton, Cummy, 31
Baun, Bobby, 68
Beliveau, Jean, 96, 132
Berenson, Red, 18–21
Bibeault, Mike, 103–104
Blair, Andy, 107
Blake, Toe, 103, 135
Bodnar, Gus, 56–60
Boston Bruins, 40, 43–46, 57, 61, 74–77, 79, 106, 138–141
Bower, Johnny, 68
Bruneteau, Mud, 80
Bucyk, Johnny, 138, 140
Buller, Hy, 57

Calder, Frank, 131
Campbell, Clarence, 63–67

Canadian Fitness Institute, 33
Canadian Junior Hockey Division, 37
"Canadian Meteor, The," 50, 53
Chabot, Lorne, 80–81
Cheevers, Gerry, 76–77, 139
Chicago Black Hawks, 52, 56, 70, 96–99, 119–121, 122–124, 127–131, 132–136
Clancy, King, 78–79, 108, 113–116
Clarke, Bobby, 40
Corrigan, Mike, 76–77
Crichton, Kyle, 106

Davidson, Bob, 103
Day, Hap, 107
Detroit Red Wings, 21, 23, 25–32, 78–81, 91–95, 96–99, 117
Dill, Bob "Killer," 85–86
Dionne, Marcel, 76, 87
Drillon, Gordie, 130
Dupont, Andre, 119–120
Dutton, Mervyn, 85

"Edmonton Express," 106, 108
Edmonton Maple Leafs, 37
Esposito, Phil, 138–139

142

Favell, Doug, 18–21
Ferguson, Elmer, 110
Fonteyn, Margot, 108
Fontinato, Lou, 25–28
Foyt, A. J., 53

Gee, George, 56, 58
Geoffrion, Bernie "Boom Boom,"
    62, 67, 122, 132
Giacomin, Eddie, 91–95
Gilmour, Lloyd, 120
"God Bless America," 41
"Golden Jet, The," 96–99
Goodfellow, Ebbie, 57
Goring, Butch, 77
Gorman, Tommy, 85–86

Hall, Glenn, 33, 82, 139
Hamilton, Reg, 104
Hart, Cecil, 49–50
Henry, Camille, 20
Hicke, Bill, 132–133
Hodge, Ken, 138
Houle, Rejcan, 70
Howe, Gordie, 25–28, 30–32, 96,
    117–119, 137–138
Howe, Sid, 21
Hull, Bobby, 68, 96, 119–121, 122–
    126

Irvin, Dick, 101

Johnson, Ching, 112–113

Karakas, Mike, 128, 131
Kilrea, Hec, 80
Kyle, Gus, 83

Lach, Elmer, 102–103
Laycoe, Hal, 62
Leswick, Tony, 83
Lindsay, Ted, 30–32

Los Angeles Forum, 74–77
Los Angeles Kings, 15, 74–77, 87
Lumley, Harry, 32

MacLeish, Rick, 40, 42
Madison Square Garden, 23, 56, 91
Mahovlich, Pete, 57
Maki, Chico, 124
Maniago, Cesare, 124
McArthur, Dalt, 133–135
McAuley, Ken, 37–38
McMahon, Mike, 103
McNally, Dr. Randall "Rand," 72
Mikita, Stan, 119–121, 123, 132–
    136
Miller, Bob, 15
Minnesota North Stars, 89
Mohns, Doug, 123
Montreal Canadiens, 18, 27, 48–
    52, 54, 57, 70, 82, 122, 132–136
Montreal Forum, 28, 49, 53–55
Montreal Herald, 110
Montreal Maroons, 78
Montreal Star, 108
Moore, Alfie, 128–131
Moore, Dickie, 132
Morenz, Howie, 48–55, 96
Mosienko, Bill, 56–60
Murray, Jim, 69

Nanne, Lou, 89–90
National Hockey League, 21, 25,
    39, 56, 85, 123, 137
Nesterenko, Eric, 32, 124–125
New York Islanders, 38
New York Rangers, 18, 23, 47, 56,
    60–61, 83, 85, 91, 117, 123
New York Rovers, 113

O'Meara, Baz, 108
Orr, Bobby, 14, 35, 96, 106, 137–
    141

Parent, Bernie, 40, 42
Park, Brad, 77
Pelé, 53
Percival, Dr. Lloyd, 33
Philadelphia Flyers, 18, 39–42
Picard, Noel, 69–70, 141
Pilous, Rudy, 135
Plager, Bob, 120–121
Plante, Jacques, 33
Probstein, Dr. J. G., 121
Punch Line, 101–104

Reaume, Mark, 32
Resch, Glenn, 38
Richard, Henri, 135
Richard, Maurice "Rocket," 62–67,
    82–86, 96, 101–105, 122, 135
Ruth, Babe, 53

Sabourin, Gary, 139
Sanderson, Derek, 138, 140
Saskatoon, Saskatchewan, 31
Sawchuk, Terry, 69
Schultz, Dave, 40
Shack, Eddie, 14, 25
Sharkey, Jack, 115
Shero, Fred, 39
Shore, Eddie, 69, 106–110
Sloan, Tod, 30
Smith, Clint, 60
Smith, Kate, 41–42
St. Louis Blues, 18, 119–121, 138–
    141
St. Marseille, Frank, 77

St. Patrick's Day riot, 65
Stanley Cup, 29–30, 40–42, 43, 47,
    49, 64, 70, 104, 107, 115, 127–
    131, 132–136, 138–141
Stapleton, Whitey, 70–73
Stewart, Bill, 128–131
Stewart, Nels, 57
Stoneking, Dan, 89
Stratford Streak, 48–49, 53

Thayer, Skip, 72, 121
Thompson, Cliff, 62
Thomson, Jim, 32
Toronto Gardens, 30
Toronto Maple Leafs, 30–32, 43–
    47, 59, 68, 79, 101–104, 107–
    109, 113, 127–131
Trottier, Bryan, 38

Udvari, Frank, 25–26

Vachon, Nicole, 88
Vachon, Rogie, 38, 75–76, 87–88
Van Impe, Ed, 18
Venasky, Vic, 38
Vezina Trophy, 91
Victoria Skating Rink, 101

Wakely, Ernie, 119–120
Washington Lions, 113
Wharram, Kenny, 123
Williams, Tommy, 77
Worsley, Gump, 33, 117–119
"Wreck Richard" Club, 85